MONEY

@

THE SPEED OF THOUGHT

JOSEPH DOLAPO OTAIKU

DEDICATION

This work is solely dedicated to God my Father whose gifting upon my life has been the reason for my existence; His ever presence with me in every ramification cannot be over emphasized. Also, to my mum, Mrs. Beatrice Otaiku; mum I say you're indeed a mother-in-Israel. Not forgetting my mentor, Bob Proctor, whom I attracted to myself during my voyage to discovering how I can live the lifestyle I desire to live; he taught me "how to" and ultimately helped me through the process of changing my "Paradigm"

CONTENTS

Dedication 2

Introduction.. 4

CHAPTER ONE:
The Color of Money...8

CHAPTER TWO:
Money and the Law of Attraction...............................17

CHAPTER THREE:
Use the Law of Attraction as your own Money Magnet.......................24

CHAPTER FOUR:
Techniques on registering your desires into your subconscious..........27

CHAPTER FIVE:
Attract Money Now with the Speed of light....................29

CHAPTER SIX:
Raising your Financial Vibration................................33

CHAPTER SEVEN:
Is becoming Rich inherently evil?..............................43

CHAPTER EIGHT:
Overcoming Cheapness..49

CHAPTER NINE:
Attract Money Now!..58

CHAPTER TEN:
Becoming an Enlightened Millionaire.........................60

CHAPTER ELEVEN:
Money and Spirituality...63

CHAPTER TWELVE:
How to Manifest Money fast using the Law of Attraction and EFT...68

CHAPTER THIRTEEN:
Is Thinking enough in Manifesting Money?....................72

CHAPTER FOURTEEN:
Ten strategies to Creating Lavish Prosperity................75

CHAPTER FIFTEEN:
Tithing...77

CHAPTER SIXTEEN:
How to use EFT to give and get more.........................82

CHAPTER SEVENTEEN:
God's Will for our Money..87

INTRODUCTION

What Is Money?

Everyone uses money. We all want it, work for it and think about it. If you don't know what money is, you are not like most humans. However, the task of defining what money is, where it comes from and what it's worth belongs to those who dedicate themselves to the discipline of economics. While the creation and growth of money seems somewhat intangible; money is the way we get the things we need and want.

Before the development of a medium of exchange, people would barter to obtain the goods and services they needed. This is basically how it worked: two individuals each possessing a commodity the other wanted or needed would enter into an agreement to trade their goods. This early form of barter, however, does not provide the transferability and divisibility that makes trading efficient. For instance, if you have cows but need bananas, you must find someone who not only has bananas but also the desire for meat. What if you find someone who has the need for meat but no bananas and can only offer you bunnies? To get your meat, he or she must find someone who has bananas and wants bunnies.

The lack of transferability of bartering for goods, as you can see, is tiring, confusing and inefficient. But that is not where the problems end: even if you find someone with whom to trade meat for bananas, you may not think a bunch of them is worth a whole cow. You would then have to devise a way to divide your cow (a messy business) and determine how many bananas you are willing to take for certain parts of your cow. To solve these problems came commodity money, which is a kind of currency based on the value of an underlying commodity. Colonialists, for example, used beaver pelts and dried corn as currency for transactions. These kinds of commodities were chosen for a number of reasons. They were widely desired and therefore valuable, but they were also durable, portable and easily stored.

Another example of commodity money is the U.S. currency before 1971, which was backed by gold. Foreign governments were able to take their U.S. currency and exchange it for gold with the U.S. Federal Reserve. If we think about this relationship between money and gold, we can gain some insight into how money gains its value: like the beaver pelts and dried corn, gold is valuable purely because people want it.

It is not necessarily useful - after all, you can't eat it, and it won't keep you warm at night, but the majority of people think it is beautiful, and they know others think it is beautiful. Gold is something you can safely believe is valuable. Before 1971, gold therefore served as a physical token of what is valuable based on people's perception.

Impressions Create Everything

The second type of money is fiat money, which does away with the need to represent a physical commodity and takes on its worth the same way gold did: by means of people's perception and faith. Fiat money was introduced because gold is a scarce resource and economies growing quickly couldn't always mine enough gold to back their money requirement. For a booming economy, the need for gold to give money value is extremely inefficient, especially when, as we already established, value is really created through people's perception.

Money then becomes the token of people's apprehension of worth - the basis for why money is created. An economy that is growing is apparently doing a good job of producing other things that are valuable to it and to other economies. Generally, the stronger the economy, the stronger its money will be perceived (and sought after) and vice versa. But, remember, this perception, although abstract, must somehow be backed by how well the economy can produce concrete things and services that people want.

That is why simply printing new money will not create wealth for a country. Money is created by a kind of a perpetual interaction between concrete things, our intangible desire for them, and our abstract faith in what has value: money is valuable because we want it, but we want it only because it can get us a desired product or service.

How is it measured?
Sure, money is the $10 bill you lent to your friend the other day and
don't expect back anytime soon. But exactly how much money is out
there and what forms does it take? Economists and investors ask this
question everyday to see whether there is inflation or deflation. To
make money more discernible for measurement purposes, they have
separated it into three categories:
M1 – This category of money includes all physical denominations of
coins and currency, demand deposits, which are checking accounts and
NOW accounts, and travelers' checks. This category of money is the
narrowest of the three and can be better visualized as the money used
to make payments.
M2 – With broader criteria, this category adds all the money found in
M1 to all time-related deposits, savings deposits, and non-institutional
money-market funds. This category represents money that can be
readily transferred into cash.
M3 – The broadest class of money, M3 combines all money found in
the M2 definition and adds to it all large time deposits, institutional
money-market funds, short-term repurchase agreements, along with
other larger liquid assets.

By adding these three categories together, we arrive at a country's
money supply, or total amount of money within an economy.

How Money is created
Now that we've discussed why and how money, a representation of
perceived value, is created in the economy, we need to touch on how
the central bank can manipulate the money supply.

Among other things, a central bank has the ability to influence the level
of a country's money supply. Let's look at a simplified example of how
this is done. If it wants to increase the amount of money in circulation,
the central bank can, of course, simply print it, but as we learned, the
physical bills are only a small part of the money supply.

Another way for the central bank to increase the money supply is to buy government fixed-income securities in the market. When the central bank buys these government securities, it puts money in the hands of the public. How does a central bank such as the Federal Reserve pay for this? As strange as it sounds, they simply create the money out of thin air and transfer it to those people selling the securities! To shrink the money supply, the central bank does the opposite and sells government securities. The money with which the buyer pays the central bank is essentially taken out of circulation. Keep in mind that we are generalizing in this example to keep things simple.

Remember, as long as people have faith in the currency, a central bank can issue more of it. But if the Fed issues too much money, the value will go down, as with anything that has a higher supply than demand. So even though technically it can create money "out of thin air," the central bank cannot simply print money as it wants.

THE COLOR OF MONEY

Like it. Loathe it. Want it. Waste it. But you just cannot ignore it. What is the value of money? That rumpled piece of printed-paper in your wallet that the world bows to its power? The secret lies in your own mind!

Let's talk money! We are talking about a piece of paper, right? A scrap created from wooden goo that wouldn't even fetch a glass of water if used for trade on the basis of its actual worth.

So what makes money tick? We love it, we condemn it. We go all out to get as much of it as we can, then we berate it for being a temptation! We live with it and realize our dreams through it, yet are the first to say 'money can't buy everything'. Why? But then, how do you evaluate the worth of something that in itself defines worth, at least commercially? Is money a capitalist weapon for exploitation? Or the most tactile evaluation and reward of our capabilities?

Perhaps it's only fair that we begin with one of the few people who actually championed money and its philosophical and ethical worth.

Value for value
"Money," is a tool of exchange, which can't exist unless there are goods produced and men able to produce them. Money is the material shape of the principle that men who wish to deal with one another must deal by trade and give value for value."

The catchphrase is 'value for value'. And, maybe, trust in a promise made on a piece of paper. In this sense, money or trade recognizes the belief that nothing in the world is free. Whatever we wish to have, has to be earned. So, if A wants what B owns, or is in a position to give, then A has to give B something of equal worth. Some believed that only those who did not want to trade would condemn money. Who wanted for free what others had created with their effort and capability.

Money has served as a medium of exchange after trying a variety of other items, which were found lacking. Every person needs products and services in life. Money plays the role of a recognized value for the exchange of commodities and services. If there was no commonly-accepted unit for these transactions, there would be anarchy in the world.

We can take a step further in recognizing money as the means of sustenance. Money is the source of survival. The verdict you pronounce upon the source of your livelihood is the verdict you pronounce upon your life. Perhaps it is worthwhile to wonder why money still draws so much flak. Why is it that most people hesitate to proclaim that they actually like money? What's the taboo all about? When did a simple tool for exchange metamorphose into an ambivalent entity that is at once a source of shame and exultation?

"The man who damns money has obtained it dishonorably; the man who respects it has earned it," proclaims Ayn Rand boldly.

Is money evil?
Remember your first salary check? And the pride you felt to have earned something? How would you have felt if somebody had pointed out that it was wrong to like money? That the pride you were feeling was evil?

A large part of this negative image has come about thanks to a misreading of the scriptures by the world's major organized religions, notably Christianity and Brahminical Hinduism. Wealth, claimed the pundits of yore, was a sin if it was not accumulated for a 'godly' purpose. Renunciation was the catchword, poverty the goal and austerity the norm of the day. If you did not practice these, you were a sinner; decreed to being either reborn as a lower animal if a Hindu, or to be barbecued in the fires of hell, if a Christian. There was, however, an easy way out. Just keep donating money to religious institutions and God would turn a blind eye to how you earn your wealth.

As Canadian Nathan Lester says: "Do you see a pattern here? Religion denounces money and then accepts 10 per cent of our earnings!"

But the scriptural truth was far from this bribe-God-be-happy image. Notes American financial consultant and inspirational author J. Grady Cash in his book Value-Based Money Management: "Money is not evil. The actual Biblical quote that leads to this common misconception is 'for the love of money is the root of all evil'. The ancient Aramaic text might more accurately be translated as 'for the lust after money is the root of all evil'. It's perfectly acceptable to want to make more money. Only when money is accumulated for its own sake or its accumulation hurts others does money become bad."

Artha, or wealth, is legitimate; money is indispensable in the present state of society. A man of the world without money is a failure; he cannot keep body and soul together. Furthermore, money is needed to build hospitals, schools, museums, and educational institutions, which distinguish a civilized society from a primitive one. Money gives leisure, a key factor in the creation of culture. But money must be earned according to dharma; otherwise it debases a man by making him greedy and cruel.

The basic issue, therefore, is not whether money is evil but whether it has been earned ethically.

The ethics of wealth

Despite knowing this, many of us still shy away from talking about it openly. As New Age guru Deepak Chopra puts it: "Most people find it difficult to tell someone exactly how much money they make. This is because they believe that they are worth only what they earn."

Why should this be so? I can simply answer this question by saying; Are you too rich if others are poor? One of our unconscious but profound beliefs about money is that it is a zero-sum game, and that for one person to have more means another has less. In short, that wealth is made on the backs of the poor. But there is an assumption here that is only partly accurate, and that is that money is a physical commodity that can be moved about like a pile of marbles. I suspect that the truth is that money has a dual nature. For if the zero-sum theory holds part of the truth of money, the other part is this: prosperity can beget prosperity.

John Stussel, host of the 20/20 American TV show episode on the positive side of greed, accurately puts it: "Bill Gates is a good example. He's now one of the world's richest men. He's got about $40 billion. But does his having $40 billion mean the rest of us have lost $40 billion? No."

According to Stussel, in a trade-driven economy even if a person is greedy for more wealth, he just can't grab it from others. "To get your money, he has to persuade you, entice you. To do that, he has to make something that you will willingly give him money for. All commerce requires both parties to benefit. Take the simple example. I buy a quart of milk from a farmwoman. I hand her the dollar; she gives me the milk. We both benefit, because she wanted the dollar more than the milk, and I wanted milk more than the dollar."

Ram Piparaiya, Chairman, Aridhi Hitech Industries, Mumbai agrees: "Money does not corrupt. It depends on the user. Corrupt people become more corrupt with it." He, however, feels that those who don't earn but win money, especially through lotteries or gambling, are more likely to be corrupted by it.

B.R. Tangri, chief manager (PR) at the Oriental Bank of Commerce, Delhi, has a pointblank response to the debate: "How can money be evil? After all, can one survive without money?"

Actually, the notion that money corrupts is itself debatable. Money, intrinsically, is a means of trade. And the person who holds more money has greater power to dictate the terms of trade. Now, we have all heard that 'power corrupts'. But does power corrupt all? What about great leaders who have had the power to shape history, yet did it with integrity and wisdom? Then, shouldn't the responsibility of not being corrupt lie with the person and not the object of temptation? "A knife can be used by a terrorist or by a surgeon," agrees Somani. "Bofors guns can be used to defend the country or get embroiled in an underhand deal. Whether money corrupts or not depends on one's attitude and character."

Your attitude towards money has a significant reflection on your attitude to life. Some people see money as a means to an end, some as a tool to wield power, some as an end in itself-thinking it will bring them happiness. A person who sees money as only a means to satisfy needs will be relaxed and more benevolent than one who craves money for providing self-worth, security or power.

Money may buy you ten yachts and five mansions. But, as the cliché goes, it really cannot buy you happiness or self-worth, for that matter. If you run after money to find what you couldn't find within, you are chasing a mirage that will only leave you more at a loss.

The right attitude
So what may be the right attitude to money? I see human-money interaction as another form of relationship and the argument that laws applicable to any other healthy relationship also govern the attitude towards money. Your individual relationship with money is similar to your relationship with yourself and others. In other words, you deal with money the same way you deal with yourself and others. Your financial relationships develop along the same energy pathways as everything else in your life.

Money is necessary for my life. Money keeps me comfortable, but it is not the only reason for my happiness. Happiness comes from within me. Money is an indicator of practical success, but not of my self-worth.

The general attitude towards money, however, is two-fold; we are either eternally running after it or are busy berating our fate for keeping us away from more of it. The grapes are eternally sour and yet we keep jumping for the ever-higher bunch. The few of us who manage to break this vicious cycle are the ones who have a good relationship with money.

One thing strongly stands that, You'll See It When You'll Believe It. At this point I need send a warning against this anomalous attitude that says; "If we have a scarcity mentality, it means that we believe in scarcity, that we evaluate our life in terms of its lacks. The theme of so many people's life is 'I simply do not have enough', or 'I would be a lot happier if I had...' People believe that they live a life of lack because they are unlucky, instead of recognizing that their belief system is rooted in scarcity thinking. Yet as long as they live with a scarcity mentality, which is what they will attract to their lives."

Most personal growth trainers, however, insist that this attitude is easily rectified. All it needs is a change in thought patterns regarding money. Money is only a state of mind; not a reality in, of, or for itself. If money remains a state of mind, therefore a spiritual reality and not an end in itself, then you always will have what you truly need and deserve.

Easier said than done, you may snort. After all, it does hurt when you see others making less effort at making money but succeeding more than you. Perhaps you could ponder on what it is that successful people do to reach where they are.

Success versus money

Like it or not, most often success is judged in terms of a person's bank balance. In a consumer-driven economy, a penchant for selling—ideas, concepts or products—goes a long way in earning money, as well as in being materially successful. "If you don't want to sell what you produce," asks Lester, "why would you produce it?" Which is why, today, even spiritual leaders and healers need to advertise their unique capabilities because the most successful are those who reach out to a wide variety of people. After all, how would a person sitting in Timbuktoo know where to go for something as esoteric as rudraksha therapy, if not through advertisements?

Despite consumerism, it would be a mistake to read success as a synonym for money. Although the two often go hand in hand, money itself cannot make you a success, and vice-versa. Take Joseph Dolapo Otaiku, founder of The Master's Colt Arena as example. A simple man who came from a not-so-well-to-do family, nobody can deny that he is a success. Yet, who is interested in how much money he makes? What makes him a success is his intellect and achievements.

What about the sages who left all to seek something much more intangible? Were they any less of a success? Would the Buddha have been more successful had he stayed with his palace and wealth?

Money rarely defines a person's worth in the real sense of the term. In an ideal world, money would change hands ethically and the money that you earn would be directly proportionate to your capability. In the real world, money is often a result of lineage, contacts, unethical shortcuts or exploitation; so that the respect it should demand in ideal circumstances eludes it.

Ambition or greed?

In the '80s, Gordon Gecko—a reptilian stockbroker played brilliantly by Michael Douglas in Oliver Stone's movie Wall Street—extolled greed thus: "The point is, ladies and gentlemen, that greed, for lack of a better word, is good. Greed is right. Greed works… Greed captures the essence of the evolutionary spirit." Like it or not, in the market-oriented world of today, Gecko might just be stating the obvious. The word greed is defined in the Oxford English Dictionary as 'intense or inordinate longing, especially for wealth or food; avarice; covetous desire'. It is the inordinate desire for wealth and affluence that has made material evolution possible. At least in terms of trade. Had we not wanted money, would we have got it in the first place?

A person who desires money desires it for a purpose. If you are greedy, you will forever covet, irrespective of how much you have. And this has nothing to do with your social or monetary status. A millionaire can be as greedy as a daily wage earner. In fact, in one of political science's greatest ironies, the twin concepts of communism and socialism-which arose from a desire to overthrow greedy capitalism-also gave in to greed in their practical application.

Gecko equated greed with ambition, with the desire to better your own self. Actually there is a subtle difference between the two, and one can easily be transmuted into the other. The difference, most often, lies in the motive. Dan Sullivan, a US-based personal growth trainer, notes: "Ambition is the desire to have more, but greed is the desire to have more at the expense of others. Ambition is natural and rational, but greed is a product of fear. Where there is no fear, there is no greed."

So, if you want money without being attached to it, you remain free of greed in spite of being in the rat race. But when you let money dictate your life, you become its slave, and in the end, money begins to rule you.

The spirit of money

So, to what extent does money define our life? Is there anything beyond money?

Interestingly, this brings two sharply contradictory theories in focus— money as the basis of trade, with which we are all concerned, and money as temptation, where the less we have to do with it, the better. How does one balance the two?

With money, things that seem fair play from one point of view turn into ethically suspect areas from other perspectives. Actually, the problem does not lie with money at all, it lies with our perspective. At its basest level, what is money? A piece of paper, a promissory note, a piece of plastic, a punched-in number on the stock market. That's it; nothing more, nothing less.

The person who amasses great wealth through hard work, and the person who gives away all in the blink of an eye share the same platform from a spiritual perspective. Both are following their dharma. Money plays but a negligible role in terms of their spiritual evolution, since money is the outcome, not the source of their perspectives on life.

"Money does not define us", says Tom. "We define what money means." And so long as our life is governed by a reliance on our swadharma, the innate correctness of action that one is born with, the money that we earn would not just benefit us, but also contribute to a better and prosperous society.

The enigma of money is a creation of our own minds. Then why get ensnared in it? It may come as a cliché to many, but we are the masters of money. Believe that—and you have money by the short and curlies!

MONEY AND THE LAW OF ATTRACTION

It was really interesting to see the full spectrum of reactions to a survey conducted by my company on the issue of "MONEY" as regards our coaching and consulting charges. I expected this would be a polarizing survey for some people, so the reactions weren't surprising. Some people said it was a mistake to charge $500 per hour because that price was way too high and would make it impossible for most people to afford, so it was an elitist and/or greedy price point. On the other hand, several people cautioned me that it was a mistake to charge $500 per hour because I would be quickly overwhelmed. They questioned my reasons for going so low. A few said they were eager to take advantage of such a bargain and that they knew others who'd be interested too. However, the undertone was that this wouldn't be a practical price point in the long run and that for my own good; I'd have to raise the price quickly.

The first form of feedback came mainly via the forums; the second was mostly via my private contact form. This didn't surprise me. The forums tend to attract a younger audience; since younger people are more comfortable using forums and tend to have more time for them, and younger people are more likely to fall into the "$500 is a huge sum" group.

What's interesting is that this feedback has little to do with the actual price. I'd have gotten the same feedback if I'd said the price was $50 or $1500. The volume of feedback on each side would shift, but there'd still be people on both sides.

How much money is a large sum?

Is $500 a large or small amount? It depends on your perspective. If you're in a scarcity mindset, it might seem like a huge sum. If you have a wealthy mindset, it may be a tiny amount. That may be hard to believe, but it's true.

I used to think $500 was a lot of money. It certainly seemed so when I would end a month with less than $100 total. If I gained or lost an extra $500, it could make a difference in my finances for months to come. An extra $500 was a significant amount of money. But after shifting my mindset about money to invite more abundance into my life, $500 began to seem like a tiny amount. $500 represents the cash I might carry in my wallet. If I gain or lose $500, it makes no real difference in my finances. $500 is a fairly insignificant amount.

Once I got my mindset to this point (which I did mostly by imagining what it would feel like to be there in reality), it wasn't long before my reality began to reflect it. I became a "vibrational match" for earning larger sums. At one point having more than $100,000 in the bank would have seemed rich or wealthy. But now it just feels normal... like duh, I'm supposed to have that much cash all the time.

Here are some examples to help shed more light on the concept of financial relativity.

A realtor thinks having $50,000 cash is normal. Shortly after I moved to Victory Garden City in 2011, we were chatting with a local realtor who said she liked to keep at least $50,000 cash on hand at all times (not for investment, just for her personal money). I gave myself a quizzical look. I thought she must be very snooty or elitist to feel that way. Why would anyone need that much cash?

Eventually I realized that my reaction to her statement was precisely why I could never save up $50,000 in cash. I was pushing it away from myself by assuming it was too much money to hold onto. Having $5,000 cash was about normal for me; $10,000 meant I was doing incredibly well.

I realized these figures were arbitrary as far as the universe is concerned, so I should be able to raise them at will. I began imagining having $50,000 cash AND considering it normal to have that much. The second part is really critical. In order to become the kind of person who could have $50,000 cash in the bank, it had to feel just plain normal to me, not fantastic or incredible. So I actually visualized seeing this sum on my bank statement and reacting with a ho hum, excitement-free response.

This might sound counter-intuitive at first, but it worked. I was able to have $50,000 cash only when I began to see it as a normal amount to have in the bank instead of a windfall. Today if I were to have only $50,000 cash on hand, I'd feel some financial pressure to raise it back up again.

Now if your reaction to my saying this is similar to how I initially reacted to that realtor, it's safe to say you're keeping yourself out of resonance to having such sums of money yourself. The big question is: Why are you doing this to yourself? Why not invite larger sums into your life instead of pushing them away? Are you suffering from low self-esteem or something?

Keep in mind that other people may be equally shocked by your opulent lifestyle even if you think it's a normal (not wealthy or excessive) place to be. There's a good chance you're a lot wealthier than most people on this planet. What may feel normal to you could be a windfall for someone else. Who are you to be able to eat whenever you're hungry or to have access to medical care when you need it? Do the expectations of others make you want to live below your potential to satisfy them? Or would you rather help those people raise their standard of living to at least the level you consider normal?

A few years ago when I was studying poker (just for fun), I watched a poker tournament on TV where Daniel Negreanu one of the "winningest" players on earth got knocked out of the final table. His prize money was $60,000. The top prize for first place was probably around $1 million. In the exit interview, he was asked what he was going to do with all the money he won. He chuckled with surprise, as if to say, "Money? What money? I lost the tournament." Then he said something like, "I dun no. $60,000? What can I do with that? Buy a car maybe? He clearly had the attitude that $60,000 was a small, almost negligible amount of money. It wasn't a serious sum.

It was as if the interviewer had said, "Daniel, you just won a dollar! What are you going to do with it?" And Daniel replied jokingly, "I dun no... buy a soda maybe? [Sigh]."

While some people might see Negreanu's attitude as haughty, arrogant, or elitist, I think it's a reflection of a wealthy mindset. This may help explain why his tournament poker winnings exceed $10 million to date. Since $60K represents a small amount to him, he's a vibrational match for earning and holding much larger sums. If $60K was a lot of money to him, he probably wouldn't be able to win even that much, and even if he did win it, he'd have a hard time holding onto it.

A businessman thinks $24,000 is a fair price for an hour of his time. Earlier this year I spent a few hours talking with a businessman who consults for $24,000 per hour. And yes, people actually pay him that amount. In a short period of time, he can help his clients optimize their businesses in such a way that this is a profitable exchange for them. If I tell him I'm charging $500 per hour for a consultation, there's a good chance he'll laugh at me as if I'm suffering from low self-esteem or something.

Is a 30-minute consultation with this man really worth as much as 24 hours of consulting with me? Does he have 48x as much business knowledge, experience, and insight as I do? Of course not. He gets paid this amount because he's a match for receiving it. To him this is normal. For me it would still seem amazing or incredible.

Becoming a match for a million-dollar home

Many years ago, I was on vacation in San Diego. At the time I was basically broke and deep in debt. I was driving around Rancho Santa Fe, a wealthy neighborhood with homes that cost a few million dollars each. As we drove past a real estate office, an idea struck me, and I wanted to have some fun.

I walked into the realtor's office and confidently proclaimed that I was interested in buying a house in Rancho Santa Fe, something in the $2-4 million range. I knew that was a reasonable price range because I had checked out the listings taped to the office window before I walked in. A realtor welcomed me and asked me a few questions. I answered honestly that I ran a software company Lagos, Nigeria. Next thing I knew, the realtor was driving me around in her Jaguar, shuttling me to various homes for sale in the area. I had a fun time pretending I could actually afford them while trying not to look like total idiots. "Hmm… that tennis court looks like it will need repaving soon."

At the time I thought this exercise would help me adopt a wealthier mindset. I'd be inspired by all the wealthy homes. But it didn't work at all. I just wasn't a match for those kinds of homes. They were too exciting to me. I couldn't imagine living there and having it feel normal. It was too big a leap… too impossible.

Fast forward about 12 years to 2011. I went shopping for a new house in Las Vegas, this time for real. Our price range was $1-2 million. I paid a little over $300,000 for my previous home, so this was a big step up. But this time when the realtor took me around, it was totally different than when I was looking at homes in Rancho Santa Fe. This time I could actually imagine living there and having it feel normal to me. I was mildly excited but not overwhelmingly so. I looked at many different homes and ended up buying my first choice.

Years ago this house would have seemed amazing or extravagant to me. But now it just feels normal to live here. It actually surprises me when people visit and seem overwhelmed or amazed by it. I certainly enjoy living here, but it isn't amazing or overwhelming to me.

Do you ever buy things for yourself that seem like normal purchases but which other people might consider an extravagant or wasteful luxury? Have you ever bought a cup of coffee or bottled water? If you buy such items regularly, you probably don't consider them luxuries. They're just normal purchases. But many people would disagree and say you're being incredibly selfish and wasteful. You don't need coffee, and you could just as easily drink tap water. You elitist pig!

My point is to demonstrate that if you think something is out of reach for you, it is. If you think it's normal or expected, it becomes so. Realize that your comfort zone is totally arbitrary though. To many people on earth, getting adequate nutrition is a luxury. To some people, a million-dollar home would be killing it. You define your own comfort zone.

Imagine having as much cash and income as you have now. Would it make you uncomfortable, at least initially, if you suddenly found yourself there — not in fantasy but in reality? Would you feel awkward, uncertain, unworthy, or anxious? What would it take for you to embrace the mindset that this higher level of abundance is perfectly normal for you?

Just because you've been conditioned to believe a certain level of wealth is normal for you doesn't mean that standard is objectively meaningful. You needn't spend the rest of your life remaining loyal to arbitrary inherited beliefs. I know it may seem counter-intuitive to aim to feel normal instead of excited when it comes to earning more money. The truth is that too much excitement will actually block you from receiving larger sums because that probably isn't how you'd feel if you were actually there.

If you think $X is a large sum, and the amount makes you anxious or excited, you simply won't be able to attract and hold $X. If you really had $X and could hold onto it easily, how would you feel about it? It would seem as normal to you as your current financial equilibrium.

In this case the proper application of the Law of Attraction is actually to dampen — not to magnify — your emotions, such that the new level you want to reach begins to feel normal, expected, and believable. Otherwise you're holding yourself in a state of disbelief. If reaching your goal seems like a miracle or a monstrous windfall, you're actually pushing it away from you. This is true not just with money but with anything else you might wish to attract, including new relationships, career advancement, spiritual development, health gains, etc.

General enthusiasm about your goals is fine, but if you're holding yourself in a state of awe and amazement when you think about them, it's a safe bet you'll never get there. If you want to enjoy more financial abundance, you must learn to become comfortable with the kinds of changes that currently make you feel uncomfortable.

USE THE LAW OF ATTRACTION AS YOUR OWN PERSONAL MONEY MAGNET

Using the Law of Attraction as your own personal money magnet is easy when you know one of the best kept "secrets" of the Law of Attraction, which is "energetic magnetism." In fact, the terms "Law of Attraction" and "energetic magnetism" could be used interchangeably since they are essentially the same. This subject explains the top two tricks that most people miss when it comes to making the Law of Attraction work for money.

If you want to be magnetic to money, you want to create the ability to draw or pull money to yourself. To do this, you want to create within yourself something called, "magnetism" and to do that, you have to think in terms of "energy" rather than just thinking in terms of cerebral pursuits such as positive thinking.

According to Google's Dictionary, magnetism is defined as, "A physical phenomenon produced by the motion of electric charge, resulting in attractive and repulsive forces between objects." While that sounds, a little too scientific for most of us, what it's basically saying is what you need to do is charge two objects with enough energy to attract to each other. In our case, since we want to manifest money with the magnetism of the Law of Attraction, the two objects which we want to "energetically charge" would be you and money. So, let's say that money already has a certain electrical charge or energy which can also be called a "frequency." Like a radio dial has numbers to indicate the different energetic frequencies of the radio channels, so does money already have a "channel" or "energetic frequency" on the dial of this planet. All you have to do is get the physical "energetic frequency" of your body (your radio dial) "tuned" to match money or whatever you desire. Although it sounds difficult, it's really rather easy when you know a couple of tricks.

What you need do when you want to learn how to attract money with the Law of Attraction using its magnetism is to think "energetically" rather than "intellectually." When you think "energetically," you've learned the true secret for using the Law of Attraction to manifest money. This is how to attract money, plain and simple, but most people don't know about this one significant factor when learning how to manifest money.

Most people approach the law of attraction thinking that it's all in their minds. But, it's not just "all in their minds." A larger part of learning how to manifest money is changing the physical "energetic" signal (frequency) that you are putting out to the Universe through your body, and you can't easily do this by just doing affirmations. You have to do it by doing things that actually change your body's energy, or frequency, to match the electrical charge or frequency of the money. When you do this, the indisputable science of magnetism takes over and you draw things to you very quickly.

One way to work "energetically" rather than "intellectually" with the Law of Attraction for money is by doing things that teach your body the physical vibration of what you want. For example, if you want more clients, then you physically pretend and go through the physical motions of acting as if you have clients. Yes, this means pretending to talk to them on the phone, making initial appointments, etc. This teaches your body the vibration or frequency of having clients and, thus makes your body charged with the identical electrical charge or frequency of having clients and, bingo, you become magnetic to having clients.

Is there more to it than that? Well, yes. You can do all the pretending that you want, but if your subconscious is fighting you, you're still "up a creek without a paddle." While this still sounds like it's in the cerebral arena, it's really in the energetic arena because your subconscious is also putting out an energetic signal at the same time you're thinking or doing other things. What you want to do is change your subconscious to also become magnetic to money and there are specific technologies you can use that teach your mind how to become magnetic to money because your subconscious is your strongest "homing pigeon" when using the Law of Attraction to manifest money. When you change your subconscious to attract money, you've given yourself the second key to unlocking the magic of the Law of Attraction for money.

If you want to use the Law of Attraction as your own personal money magnet, use the absolute power of its magnetism by doing energetic exercises that change your body's physical vibration to match that which you desire, as well as using today's technologies such as targeted hypnosis and specific brainwave meditations to turn your subconscious into your own personal money magnet "homing pigeon" to automatically attract everything you desire.

TECHNIQUES ON REGISTERING YOUR DESIRES INTO YOUR SUBCONSCIOUS

In the previous chapter I mentioned some technologies that would help in bringing the subconscious mind into harmony with your desires; this will be expounded here. There is a good chance that you have already heard about what the law of attraction is. It is a law that states that we attract whatever we think about the most, in our life. So this means, if we think about elephants all day, we will somehow attract elephants in our life! This also means that we can knowingly attract almost anything we desire - money, world travel, love etc. if we think about our desire intensely for some time. However, do you know exactly how to use the law of attraction to manifest reality? In this chapter, we will discuss the exact steps to be taken to manifest anything using the law of attraction.

Steps:
1. Sit or lie down in a calm place where you won't be disturbed. Close your eyes and try to focus on your breathing. Relax.
2. Now, for about half a minute (30 seconds), clearly visualize already having exactly what you desire. For example, if you want a new car, visualize yourself already having the new car. Try feeling how you would feel if you somehow got that new car. Touch your new car. Drive it. Enjoy that feeling of joy you will experience when you drive your new car. The point is: try creating the exact experience of your desire being fulfilled in your mind.
3. After about half a minute, Stop! Smile and forget about the visualization. Go about your activities for the day and try not to think much about what you visualized. This is because if you dwell too much upon your desire, there is a good chance that you will think negative thoughts about it. For example, you might think - "Will I really get my car?" or "With my current financial situation, how can I get a car?". All those thoughts will stop your manifestation. So it is best to involve yourself in other activities and forget about your desire for sometime after your visualization.

4. On the next day, again visualize your desire coming true for 30 seconds as mentioned in step 2. Close your eyes, relax and clearly feel the feeling of excitement and happiness as you see your desire coming true in your imagination. Then again, after the visualization, forget about it and focus on other work. Repeat this "visualization" process for some day.

5. If you have followed the process correctly, very soon an unbelievable opportunity related to a new car or whatever your desire is will manifest. You might suddenly get a fantastic deal on the car you've always wanted. Or you might "win" the car of your dreams in a lottery. The law of attraction works in interesting ways.

After you have visualized your desire coming true, you might be tempted to think more about it throughout the day. You can think about it, but make sure whatever you think is extremely positive and supports what you have visualized. If you feel you have started thinking thoughts like - "of course this won't work" or "there is no way my desire can be fulfilled", then, stop, lie down or relax and visualize for 30 seconds again - until you feel excited about your desire actually being fulfilled.

Sometimes, it can be difficult to manifest large desires directly because we are very emotionally attached to them and so think negative thoughts about them very frequently. So you can try this technique to initially manifest small desires like "ice cream", "a book you want", "a mobile phone" etc. You could experiment with small desires and later move on to big desires.

Warnings:
No matter what happens, DON'T think about negative things related to your desire after visualizing. Note that if you think thoughts like, "This won't work" or "it's just not possible", your desire will not come true.

ATTRACT MONEY NOW WITH THE SPEED OF LIGHT

Using the law of attraction for money and wealth is incredibly easy and effective. The law of attraction says we attract the same energy we put out. All of our thoughts are energy, and therefore create and manifest our experiences. When we think, for instance, that we need money and don't have enough of it, we tend to attract that need and desperation even more. On the other hand, when we think of money as something that is available and we believe in our own power to bring more money into our lives, we immediately attract it to us. It is that simple.

Most of us can't help but worry about our finances. We need money for just about everything, and, it seems, as quick as we can make it, we find things to spend it on. This makes it very difficult to stay ahead financially, and tends to give us even more reason to fret about our bank accounts. Unfortunately, this creates a damaging cycle, in which our fears and worries about money actually create more scarcity – which creates more fears and worries. If we are ever going to break this, we need to actually take control of our thoughts and deep inner beliefs and start making positive statements about money and wealth.

Affirmations for money are one wonderful way to break through fears, worries, and negative thoughts and start attracting more wealth and material stability. Many of us are tempted to say what we want or what we need, however, this just causes us to keep wanting and needing. Instead, if we really want and need something, we have to first, be grateful for what we have already, and, second, be trusting toward the Universe. We must release desperation and fear, and the way to do that is to turn our worries into positive statements. No more saying "I want" or "I need"; instead, we say "I have," or, "I can get." Even if this is difficult to believe at first, the more we tell ourselves that money is available to us and there is no need for worry, the more we believe it, and, best of all, the more likely that it will happen.

The next thing is to consider your mindset if it is fixed on abundance or lack; but first, we will need consider the abundance mindset.

The abundance mindset

Considering the mindset that balks at seeing someone spend $10,000 for a hotel room stay; it's the mindset that would label this an extravagant or wasteful purchase. I believe this mindset is a huge mistake.

If the $10K hotel room seems like an extravagant expense, it means you're out of alignment with the mindset that is capable of producing $10K of value very quickly. It's not the expensive room itself that helps you contribute. What helps you contribute is thinking about what it would take to become the kind of person who could afford to stay in a $10K hotel room without thinking twice about it — because that's a person who's capable of generating massive value very efficiently.

At an average level of income in the USA, there's not much difference between a dime and a penny, right? It is a small amount both way and not particularly significant. Would you fret over a price difference of 9 cents? Hopefully not. But for some people on this planet, 9 cents is a fair amount, and to pay a dime instead of a penny for something would be regarded as extravagant and wasteful.

Similarly, at higher levels of income and value creation, $10K is nothing. It's just a penny. It's insignificant. There's virtually no difference between a $10K hotel room and a $100 hotel room — the price difference is meaningless, so why not pay that extra "9 cents" for a nicer setup?

The point is that if you harbor the outrage mindset towards "extravagant" purchases, you're keeping yourself out of alignment with becoming the kind of person who could generate that much value easily. Hence, you're severely limiting yourself and very unnecessarily.

If you want to look at it from the opposite angle, start applying what I call an "outrage script" whenever you see people overpaying a few pennies for a purchase. You could have bought that apple for 5 cents less at the store down the street! You must have money to burn!" They'll think you've lost your mind. Similarly, this is how very wealthy people think about the price difference between a $10,000 vs. a $100 hotel room. If you were to complain that they should stay in a cheaper room to save $9900, they might look at you like you're nuts.

Fretting over pennies probably seems foolish to you. Similarly, to those who are capable of generating massive value and being paid accordingly, fretting over $10K is equally foolish. People who can spend $10K on a hotel room know that $10K is not a lot of money.

I believe the outrage script is a big mistake. It holds people back more than they know, and my intention was to try to shed some light on that. If you think any amount of money is "a lot" or "too much" or "extravagant," you're resonating with scarcity, not abundance, and you're preventing yourself from becoming the kind of person who can generate that level of value. Why do this to yourself? Why hold back if you're capable of contributing so much more?

It was this realization that helped me increase my own income several times over during the past year alone and I didn't have to work harder or longer to do it. I realized that if I think of some arbitrary amount of money as huge or extravagant, whether it's $10K or $10 million, then I'm out of alignment with being able to earn that much money, which means I'm out of alignment with being able to generate that much value for others.

Remember that money is social debt. The size of your bank account is a measure of how much society owes you for the value you've already contributed. If you think $10K is a large sum, it means you probably aren't in a position to generate $10K of value for others very easily. If you can dump that unhealthy mindset, you can open yourself to generating far more value in much less time. When I started thinking of $10K as a small sum, I soon found it very easy to earn $10K. Earning $10K is about as difficult as making a sandwich.

Start where you are, and stretch yourself to let go of those limiting beliefs that hold you back. If you think it's fairly easy to earn $10 or 100, try to open your mind to the possibility that maybe, just maybe, it could be equally easy maybe even easier to earn $500 in the same amount of time or less. Once you've reached that point, push on to $1,000, and keep going from there. When you think that a certain amount of money is "no big whoop," you'll find a way to earn that much, and that means you'll be contributing more value to others. The money you receive as compensation is your receipt.

RAISING YOUR FINANCIAL VIBRATION

In this chapter, I'll share some practical tips for raising your financial vibration and expanding your financial comfort zone. If you dislike the term vibration, don't worry about it — it's arbitrary anyway. Feel free to substitute other words like acuity, prowess, intelligence, or even results.

Over time we tend to fall into financial patterns that generate a fairly narrow range of results. We become comfortable with certain financial experiences; even if we don't like those experiences, they're familiar to us, so we gravitate back to them.

In order to raise your financial vibration and improve your results, you have to shift your comfort zone. This normally requires pushing yourself through a period of discomfort. You must release the familiar to experience the unfamiliar.

Here are the basic steps to follow:
1. Assess your current financial comfort zone.
   Answer the following questions as honestly as you can:
   a. What level or range of income feels comfortable and normal to you, neither being stressfully scarce or excitedly abundant?
   b. What's the income level where you'd start to worry if you fell below it?
   c. What's the income level where you'd start to get excited if you rose above it?
   d. What amount or range of cash feels comfortable and normal to you, neither being stressfully scarce or excitedly abundant?
   e. What's the cash amount where you'd start to worry if you fell below it?
   f. What's the cash amount where you'd start to get excited if you rose above it?

For example, you might define your income comfort zone as $30,000 to $50,000 per year. And perhaps your cash comfort zone is $2,000 to $8,000. Your own figures may vary wildly from these amounts. The only correct answer is whatever feels right to you.

Don't worry about being super-precise here. Obviously there's some guesstimation involved, but try to come up with specific figures to answer these questions. Your goal is simply to get a clearer picture of your current financial equilibrium. You could have negative numbers here too if being in debt or experiencing a negative cash flow falls within your current comfort zone.

Your answers define your present financial equilibrium. You'll tend to gravitate to this range whenever you step outside it. When you fall below each range, you'll be driven to work harder to get back up again. If you start reaching the high end, you'll be hitting the edge of your comfort zone and will tend to slide back down again often via self-sabotage or slacking off.

2. Define your new financial comfort zone.
    Review your answers to the questions in the previous section. Now realize that these figures are totally arbitrary. You probably fell into these patterns based on what you learned from other people. If you had wealthy mentors, your figures are probably higher than most people. If you surround yourself with people who are broke or in debt, your figures are probably on the low side. Ultimately these amounts are under your control. You can change them if you want. You can choose to stop reinforcing the old comfort zone and push beyond it.

    Now define a new equilibrium you'd like to reach. There's no right or wrong answer, but I recommend doubling every number as a good step. When I want to reach a new level, I usually aim for a 3-5x increase because I like to push myself. If it takes me a few years to get there, I'm okay with that. It's a fun challenge to tackle.

3. Clarify and accept the consequences of your new financial vibration. Imagine what it would be like to be at your new levels, not in fantasy but in actual reality. How would this affect your lifestyle? What consequences and side effects can you imagine? Can you accept those consequences? For example, will you need to start making new friends because you can see that some people will hold you back or react negatively if you start doing better financially?

I lost a few friends as my finances improved. Some people started acting really weird around me, and it became obvious that they had major limiting beliefs about money, so I let them go. Then I attracted new friends who weren't so blocked in this area. This isn't a bad thing per se; it's just a shift you'll need to deal with.

It's very important to spend some time visualizing what your lifestyle will be like after you shift your financial equilibrium. Imagine going through your daily routine in your new reality. You might be excited at first, but there are always trade-offs. Can you accept all the natural consequences? For example, can you handle paying a lot more taxes? If you double your income, your taxes may be more than double. Do you anticipate any problems in your social network? Do you expect that a career change would be necessary, and can you handle that?

If you can't accept the consequences and side effects of your new financial equilibrium, it's extremely likely that you'll make no progress in this area. The gravitational pull of your current comfort zone will be too strong.

4. Break your old comfort zone, and build scaffolding to support your new equilibrium. Now we're getting into the action phase to initiate the shift.

A very effective way to escape your old comfort zone is to change the scaffolding of your life. This requires only a temporary burst of self-discipline instead of having to push you every day. If you have to push yourself hard every day, you'll probably fail to complete the shift. A better approach is to make changes to your environment that break your old patterns and begin conditioning new ones.

If you detect that any parts of your reality would conflict with greater financial abundance, you must break them, drop them, or leave them behind. If you want to orbit a new financial planet, you must escape the gravity of your current planet. You don't have to get every detail perfect. You just have to achieve a tipping point where you stop resonating with the old levels and start resonating with the new ones. This is where you start saying, "I quit" to anything that isn't consistent with your new levels. If you're in a dead-end job that can't possibly help you reach your new equilibrium, set a deadline for quitting. If it's clear that your job will only reinforce your old equilibrium, there's no point in pretending you can stay. You don't have to quit right away, but you do need to accept that you'll eventually have to quit.

You don't have to stress yourself over the big changes right away. Start with the easy changes first, especially those that are low-risk. Don't spend money you don't have, but do be creative in altering your environment, especially your home and your social network. Start reinforcing the new equilibrium more than the old one. This is a good time to clean house. Dump all the old junk that's inconsistent with your new equilibrium.

Review your social network, and start unplugging yourself from relationships that you know will be unsupportive after your shift. Then start building bridges with people you expect will help support you after your shift. This doesn't necessarily mean that you have to make wealthier friends. It just means you need to weaken the bonds with people who would resist your financial growth and strengthen the bonds with people who will support you.

Make a list of other changes you'll implement as more money begins to flow into your life, such as upgrading your computer, overhauling your wardrobe, taking a nice vacation, or buying more organic produce. Imagine that those things are becoming part of your daily routine. Implement those changes when you can afford to.

As you make small shifts one by one, you'll build momentum. The support structure for your old comfort zone will eventually crumble, and you'll gradually create scaffolding for your new comfort zone. If you find it too difficult to implement real changes because of too little time or money, then make the changes symbolically.
For example, you can draw or cut out pictures that represent your new equilibrium, and then post them on your walls. One time when I wanted to increase my income, I put a small fountain in my office and said to the universe, "This is my wealth fountain. It represents the flow of more money into my life in exchange for the flow of information and ideas I'm giving to others." Then I put other objects around the fountain that represented abundance and growth to me, such as a couple of plants. My income shot up rapidly during that time.

By the time you've completed this step, you should feel that you've burned the ships behind you and that there's no turning back. This doesn't mean burning the food and supplies too! It simply means that you're clearly committed to moving forward. There should definitely be some pain if you try to slink back to your old comfort zone. For example, you may endure some humiliation for begging your old friends to take you back after telling them you have to let them go.

5. Take inspired action.
    As you continue to work on #4, your old comfort zone will begin to feel less and less comfortable. You'll start feeling more congruent with your new equilibrium, even though you may not see any evidence of it in your reality yet. You might be making $50,000 per year, and even though you've been comfortable near that level for years, now it feels uncomfortably low to you. You start feeling a pressure to make more money. $100,000 per year seems like it would be a lot more comfortable to you.

When I experience this positive pressure, it feels similar to sexual arousal. It's like I have this pent-up energy inside that needs to be released. It's actually a good feeling, more like eustress than stress. The release of this energy is the eventual manifestation of my desires. When the energy is strong enough, there's a sense of inevitability about it. You can just feel you're going to get there. It's as if the manifestation is out of your hands now because the universe is working on it behind the scenes.

For example, I have this sense of inevitability that my books will become bestsellers before June 30th as a record breaking sales will be done with my books; precisely, selling 10 billion copies. It hasn't happened yet, but I can trust that it will happen. I feel the presence of a lot of pressure that needs to be released. When my book finally becomes bestsellers, I'll probably feel relieved. The pent-up energy will finally flow into physical form.

This is how it feels right before you transition to a new financial equilibrium. There's this build-up of pressure, and you sense it needs to be released. If you aren't at this point, keep working on step 4 until you get there. You simply haven't created enough arousal yet. At this point you're ready to take some inspired action. Generally the way this happens is that you'll start noticing new opportunities that are consistent with your new equilibrium. Your new energy level will attract them into your life. You'll notice new ways to earn more money.

You don't have to take major risks. Just start acting on the opportunities that present themselves. Your intentions will manifest in the form of opportunities, but you need to actively seize those opportunities. When it finally comes, your final shift can occur pretty rapidly. One week you're feeling the positive pressure, and the next week the pressure has been released, and your equilibrium has already shifted.

Focus on the opportunities that allow you to create more value for others. Realize that making more money isn't selfish. It's actually incredibly generous, assuming that you earn income by contributing equal or greater value as opposed to stealing or mooching off others.

If you double your income, it means you're contributing twice as much value to others. The money you earn is an IOU from society. If you have a million dollars in the bank, it means you've given at least a million dollars more value than you received — that's very generous. If you're in debt, it means you're taking more than you're giving. The more value you contribute, the more society owes you in return. If you allow your income to stagnate, it means you're holding back on the contribution side. That's lazy and selfish. Focus on expanding your contribution, and you'll find that society gives you a lot more IOU's.

6. Enjoy the results.
    When you successfully alter your financial equilibrium, allow yourself to feel grateful for the shift. Embrace the new possibilities and lifestyle changes you can create. Genuine gratitude will help you lock- in the changes and prevent you from backsliding. It may take a while to become comfortable with your new financial position. Don't panic! Just relax and enjoy the ride.

Growth tends to occur in quantum leaps. It's unusual to experience steady linear growth for an extended period of time. What seems like linear growth is often just a form of stagnation. For example, you may get an annual raise that barely compensates for inflation, tax increases, and other expenses, but your lifestyle remains relatively fixed because you didn't increase your contribution. If you want to experience a new level, you must be the one to initiate and sustain the shift. The point of hitting different financial tiers is to experience them fully and to learn and grow from your experiences. Once you've absorbed the key lessons of a certain level, you're ready to progress to a new level. You're in charge of the pacing.

For me the major growth lessons haven't been on the side of attracting and spending more money — or even embracing more abundance — they've been on the side of finding my true voice and learning to create and share more value. While I agree you can create shifts by focusing on the lifestyle gains, most of my personal breakthroughs have been on the side of creative self-expression. I had to tear down my old comfort zone of being at a certain level of contribution and pass through the uncomfortable zone of stepping up to a new level.

For example, I'm currently going through the shift from blogger to publish author. I can't really say how this will impact my income it obviously can't hurt, but the biggest part of this shift occurred in my sense of creative self-expression. I had to go through the steps above to create a sense of positive pressure to write a book. I didn't have to do that. I could have stuck to my old comfort zone as a blogger.

For step 3 I had to ask myself, do I really want to be an author? It was reasonable to assume that my book would get a lot of attention because of my blog. Did I really want that? How would my friends react if I became a published author? Would that bother anyone such as people who talks about writing their book someday but never follow through on it? Did I really want more email, more interview requests, and more scrutiny? It took me a while to reach the place where I was willing to accept the natural consequences of this shift.

For step 4 I made a number of small changes to shift my comfort zone. I gave myself permission to blog less often, so I could have more time for my book. I created a chapter outline on my office wall from about 200 colored sticky notes, so whenever I sat at my desk, I couldn't help but notice the rainbow-colored wall in front of me, a constant reminder to work on my book. I told my friends I was writing a book, so they'd always ask me about it. I blogged about it too. That created more accountability and helped burn the bridge behind me. It would have been more uncomfortable not to write the book.

As I created this positive pressure to write my book, opportunities began coming to me. Eventually I got an offer from Hay House and negotiated a publishing deal with them. It all went pretty smoothly because I'd shifted my equilibrium. By the time they approached me, I was ready to become an author. The opportunities came to me, but I still had to act on them. That took a lot of work, but by this point there was no turning back. That was step 5.

Step 6 is still pending. The result that excites me the most is learning how people apply the book's ideas to solve problems and make improvements in their lives. I'm not worried about whether or not everyone likes it; I accept that I can't please everyone. But I can anticipate that these ideas will generate positive results for many people because that's the effect I've experienced. Not a day goes by where I don't consciously and deliberately apply the principles in the book.

So when you seek to raise your financial vibration, realize that it isn't just about attracting more money and experiencing more abundance. Pay special attention to the contribution side as well. If you want to double your income, think about doubling your value output. How can you increase your contribution? The simple answer is that you either need to serve more people, or you need to deliver more value to each person you serve — or both. Can you go deeper? Can you go broader?

For example, writing a book allows me to go deeper and broader. It goes much deeper than any article or series of articles I've written. Secondly, by expanding into an offline medium, I can get these ideas into the hands of a lot more people than I can reach with my blog. People who've never heard of my blog will be able to find the book on Amazon.com; as well as on Kindle, including non-English translations in various countries.

You can create these kinds of shifts even if you work at a regular corporate job. You just have to think about putting yourself in a position where you can contribute more value to the people you serve which is deeper, or where you have the leverage to positively impact more people that is broader. This may be done by shifting to a more leveraged position within your current company, or it may require switching companies. You might even start your own business. You have many options, but you must be the one to initiate the shift beyond your current comfort zone.

The word comfort might sound, well, comforting. But too much comfort for too long is not a good thing. I encourage you to view comfort not as an accomplishment but rather as a state of decline. If you are too comfortable, you're coasting downhill. You're slowly dying on the inside, while something inside you longs to experience passion and excitement once again.

Instead of long-term comfort, aim for growth. Focus on increasing and expanding your contribution, and your rewards will naturally follow. When considered in isolation, a major financial gain isn't a reward that's worthy of you. It's a hollow victory that can comfort your body, but it cannot stir your soul. The soul-stirring reward is looking back on your life with deep gratitude for all the growth experiences you enjoyed as well as those you endured and feeling lovingly connected to all the people whose lives were made a little bit better by your presence.

IS BECOMING RICH INHERENTLY EVIL?

"He continued to prosper and became a very rich man".

Is it morally wrong to attempt to become rich?

It's no surprise to me that whenever the issue of money is being spoken tabled for discussion, lots of opinions tend to be initiated; while mostly getting a highly positive reception, I also uncovered some opposition from people who believe the pursuit of financial wealth is inherently greedy, selfish, immoral, or just plain evil.

How do you feel about the whole idea of having more money than you need? A lot more. Excess cash. Does that concept excite you or make you feel uncomfortable? Is it attractive or repulsive? A mixture of both perhaps? Do you feel you'd have to compromise your integrity in order to achieve this goal?

What about earning money very quickly? A fast turnover; making a quick cash. Does that raise some level of indignation within you?

If a friend were to say to you; "You know what; I'm going to go ahead and become rich," how would you react? Would you assume this person has become a "sell out" or is about to compromise their integrity? Would you ridicule them for even setting this goal? How would you feel after they achieved the goal? How would you feel if they failed and gave up?

Isn't it interesting to witness the complex feelings that arise when we examine our beliefs about money? Notice that I haven't even addressed the actual process of acquiring money in any of these situations, merely the notion of wealth itself. What role does intention play in the pursuit of wealth? Is the very idea of intending to be wealthy inherently evil, corrupt, or somehow wrong? Or can one become wealthy and still have integrity?

The level of "good" or "evil" you associate to money comes from your own beliefs and intentions, not from any innate quality that money possesses. By itself money is neutral and powerless. Your own thoughts will serve to define the role of money in your life.

If money or wealth is somehow connected with evil, greed, or selfishness in your mind, imagine what effect that will have on your financial decisions. Sounds like a good way of preventing yourself from ever becoming wealthy, doesn't it? Is that a choice you've made consciously? Do you feel it's the right one?

It isn't money or the pursuit of money that has any moral connection — you might as well be collecting rocks, beads, or sea shells. It's the energy you bring to money that matters. Money will play the role in your life that you intend it to play, and that intention will largely arise from your pre-conditioned beliefs. If you've been conditioned to associate negative qualities to money; especially through your upbringing, then money will play a largely negative role in your life. If you associate positive beliefs to money, then it will play a positive role.

But most likely you have mixed associations to money because socially conditioned beliefs are inherently incongruent — it's a case of too many cooks spoiling the broth. Your concept of money develops mixed associations to both good and evil. You want more money for yourself, but not too much more. You step towards greater wealth and then back away from it. You dance around money for fear it might be dangerous to acquire too much of it, but then when scarcity overwhelms you, you think of little else. Eventually you figure you're better off thinking about money as little as possible.

Been there, done that. It's all so much nonsense.

Your money will derive its energy from you, from who you are as a person. Greater and greater wealth will simply squeeze out more of who you already are. If what's inside you is good and noble and of high integrity, that's what will come out. But if what's inside you is fearful and uncertain, then fear and uncertainty will come out.

If you feel good about yourself, your thoughts, and your behavior, then having more money will only enhance those positive feelings and help you spread them to others.

What are you doing to earn money right now? Is your work devoted to the highest good of all? Or have you put yourself in a situation where you're earning money in such a way that's neutral or negative? Do you make money by creating or by competing? Are you giving your best value to the world or trying to get a free ride on the value creation of others?

We all grow up with a mixed bag of socially conditioned beliefs about money, especially from the media. By the time we're working adults, we become bogged down with the heavy baggage of these limiting beliefs, causing us to behave very strangely and in-congruently. Think about it for a moment… how rational is your financial behavior right now? Would an outside observer describe your financial decisions as truly intelligent and congruent when taking a deep look into your income, expenses, assets, and liabilities? Do you earn and spend money intelligently?

The only way out of the quagmire of limiting beliefs is to step back, uncover such beliefs one by one, and then consciously decide whether or not they'll continue to be true for you.

Is money the root of all evil? Is the love of money the root of all evil? Or will money simply take root in the soil of your own thoughts? Does making money quickly imply greed and selfishness? Or is it just being efficient and intelligent? Does making extra money mean that someone else loses (scarcity mentality)? Or can you make money while simultaneously increasing the wealth of others without hurting anyone (abundance mentality)? Is it intelligent to make only enough money to survive and cover your basic needs? Or is that really just being lazy and uninspired?

Have wealthy people compromised their integrity? Or is it possible to genuinely pursue greater wealth in a manner that serves the highest good of all? Is the best way to fight poverty to give more cash to people who possess a deep-seated scarcity mentality? Or is it better to challenge this mindset and plant the seeds of abundance in their thoughts?

In order to acquire greater wealth, is it necessary for you to take more than you give? Or can you become wealthy by giving much more value than you receive in return? How many wealthy people do you know intimately as opposed to through sensationalized media stories? What is their motivation?

If you had absolute financial abundance, what would you do with it? If that money were to allow you to express more of who you already are right now, what would you express? A noble purpose? The need for security? Fear and uncertainty? Self-sacrifice? Abundance and increase?

If you become wealthy and then teach hundreds of other people to do the same, have you done them a disservice and corrupted them? Or have you given them a tremendous gift?
Did you ever conclude that becoming wealthy would be out of your grasp? Have you ever thought about changing that belief?

These are all questions to consider when deciding what role money will play in your life.

One of my favorite quotes about money comes from the late, great Earl Nightingale: "Nothing can take the place of money in the area in which money works".

So amazingly accurate when you take the time to think about it.

I've had to face down a lot of these incongruencies within myself. What role is money to play in my life? Should I earn just enough to get by? Should I aim for financial independence? Do I serve people best by being broke, by earning just enough to cover my expenses, by achieving financial independence, by getting rich quickly?

Eventually I decided that it would be a good thing for me to become wealthy. Given that my purpose is to grow and to help others grow, I cannot ignore the financial dimension of personal development. If I become financially wealthy, then through my purpose I'll naturally strive to help others do the same.

Working on my wealth is really no different than working on my self-discipline, my health, my productivity, my relationships, etc. Once I made this decision, the first thing I had to do was to purge all those limiting beliefs about money from my psyche. I found quite a bit of rubbish in there, and I just let it go and decided that I would find a way to be wealthy that would be congruent with the highest good of all. Then I took some time to adopt more empowering beliefs about wealth and money.

Can achieving greater wealth for myself serve the greater good? I definitely believe this is possible. My crave for multiple sources of income allowed me to spend my time writing and posting of articles without charging for them. I was able to spend months working full-time on this new career before I earned a dime from it
But is it intelligent for me to give and give and give until I've exhausted myself through self-sacrifice? Or is it better to strike a balance between giving and receiving? What if I can help generate millions of dollars in extra wealth for others? Would it then be fair for me to share in that abundance as well?

When I write about productivity, there's a bounce back reflection that increases my own productivity. Whenever I focus on giving, I end up receiving as well. Should I block that reflection? I think that would be a mistake. I've seen how this very reflection feeds right back into the giving side, creating a positive loop of giving and receiving. But the focus has to be on the giving side, while remaining grateful for anything that comes via the receiving side. Whenever I remember to do that, I find that my own good and the highest good of all are perfectly congruent.

My intention for becoming wealthy is to do so in a manner that serves the highest good of all. I'm not going to compromise on that. If this intention meets with the universe's approval, it will manifest. If not, it won't. My current interpretation of this ideal is to work to help other people become wealthy, as one of many dimensions in which I strive to help people grow. I don't accept the scarcity model that says I must acquire wealth by taking it from others. I choose to follow the abundance model that says I can acquire wealth by creating even greater wealth for others. I genuinely believe that.

However, if you harbor serious negative associations to wealth that cause you to regard this whole concept as evil, then you should probably write me off and be done with me. You certainly won't be the first or the last person to do so. But if you choose to continue on this journey with me, be aware that I intend to help you increase your financial abundance as I do the same for myself, striving to do so in a manner that serves the highest good of all with congruency, not compromise.

OVERCOMING CHEAPNESS

For much of my adult life, I didn't have a lot of money, sometimes less than $100 cash and bank balances combined. I always seemed to be able to afford the basics of life, and I learned to be very frugal financially, meaning that I got used to being cheap.

I bought cheap food in bulk; I used to eat a lot of ramen noodles. When I needed furniture for my home office, I bought the cheapest particle-board furniture I could find and assembled it myself. I bought cheap shoes from Payless. I got hand-me-downs from relatives. I wouldn't always buy the cheapest items available, but I tried to get the best value as I perceived it. I didn't want to overpay for anything.

This felt good to me in general. I liked that I was conserving cash and making my money last. My needs were adequately met. Even as my income increased and I could afford better quality, this habit continued for a while.

Reconsidering value
One day I was browsing the bookstore, and I came across a story from Donald Trump. He noted that he used to be very value-conscious; that is cheap like me when buying clothes. That was a long time ago, so I'll paraphrase the story as best as I can remember.

Donald thought it seemed wasteful to spend $1000 on a pair of shoes when a $100 pair was just fine. The same goes for expensive suits. But he could easily afford the more expensive items. So, one day he decided to buy a pair of those super-expensive shoes. To cut to the chase, he found them to be of significantly higher quality in ways that surprised him, so much so that he questioned whether they were perhaps the better value all along.

That story struck a chord in me for some reason. It made me curious. I began to wonder if some of the more expensive items I'd been shunning were actually a better value in the long run.

I had to admit that many of the cheap items I'd bought in accordance with my value-conscious mindset often didn't last very long. The cheap shoes I bought always wore out in 6-12 months. It was pretty impressive if they lasted a full year. Cheap appliances typically broke within the first few years if I used them regularly, sometimes sooner. I ended up throwing many items away and replacing them.

Every year or two I had to buy a new wristwatch. I wondered if those cheap items were intentionally designed to break down after a certain while. I also considered that there were other areas of my life where I wasn't as cheap, and I noticed that I got better performance in those areas.

For example, one area where I wasn't cheap was computer equipment. In college I bought the best PC I could afford, a 486-DX 50 MHz with a 250MB hard drive and a Super VGA monitor. I think I paid around $2500 for it cash, not credit, which was a lot of money for me at the time. I could have spent less than $1000 for an adequate machine. I also splurged for the Borland C++ developer package instead of the much cheaper Turbo C++.

As I reflected on my various consumer experiences, I began wondering if I was being too cheap overall. Perhaps I was missing other opportunities by focusing too much on saving money.

Understanding lifetime value

Later in life I began to experiment. I figured I could afford to spend a little more money on the basics, if only to satisfy my curiosity about the difference in quality. Instead of buying shoes for $30 or less, I bought shoes that were $90+. This meant I could afford shoes that were made without animal-derived materials. Those were the most durable shoes I've ever bought. I have a pair of tennis shoes that's around 4-5 years old now, and I wear them often. They're starting to look run down, but they're still in reasonable shape. A pair of $90 sandals I bought at the same time still looks almost new. I'll probably get another 10 years of use out of them if not more.

To my surprise these "extravagant" purchases actually saved me money in the long run. If I stuck with the cheaper options, I'd have gone through 5-10 pairs of tennis shoes and probably a few pairs of sandals by now.

Buying what you truly want vs. compromising
How often do you buy what you really, truly want regardless of price? How often do you compromise and sacrifice what you want to get something cheaper? What would happen if you stopped fussing over price tags and started buying exactly what you wanted regardless of cost?

When I moved into my current home recently, I bought some new furniture. Instead of going cheap or looking for the best possible value, I decided to identify what I really wanted, regardless of price, and then as long as I could reasonably afford it, I'd buy it. Fortunately it was easy for me to agree on every item, as I seem to have similar tastes in furniture.

I didn't have limitless cash, so I gave myself a furniture budget, and once it was gone, I'd be done buying furniture for a while. If that meant I couldn't buy all the furnishings I wanted, I was okay with that. I figured I'd rather have less furniture and buy only those items I really wanted instead of filling my home with compromises. I could always buy more furniture later once I replenished my cash.

At one furniture store I bought their most expensive dining room set with a beautiful marble table top. I also bought one of their most expensive bedroom sets with the very best mattress I tested. The commissioned salesman who helped me was practically having an orgasm. I overheard him excitedly telling one of his buddies, "These guy is buying all the most expensive stuff!"

This was the first time I bought the type of furnishings that I really, really wanted — without compromising. If one item was $500 less than a comparable item that seemed a little bit nicer to me, I'd spend the extra money and buy whichever item I liked best, regardless of cost.

I couldn't afford to furnish my entire home that way without depleting my cash to an uncomfortable level or going into debt, so I left some areas of my home very sparsely furnished. If I had bought furniture using my old value-driven mindset, I'd have easily been able to furnish and decorate the entire house, but it would have been filled with compromises.

This was a very interesting experience for me. When the furniture was delivered and set up in my home, I noticed that I felt much differently about it vs. how I used to feel about all my old hand-me-down furniture. I felt so appreciative of it. I was very grateful for it.

When I used to compromise and go for value purchases, I'd never have these strong feelings of appreciation and gratitude when I got the items home. Why should I be grateful for something I didn't really want? If the item was just okay but not great, I'd end up taking it for granted. It was just a thing to be possessed.

But when I buy what I really want, regardless of how much it costs, I feel a special connection to the item. It feels good to have it around. It gives rise to feelings of abundance. It feels like a manifestation of my desires, not a consumer purchase.

<u>Enjoying abundance</u>
What do you think it's like to live in a home that's filled with stuff you really want? Well, I'll tell you; it's wonderful. It feels very abundant. Whenever I walk around my home, it's like the furniture is broadcasting positive affirmations. You can fulfill your desires; you deserve abundance. You are successful. Life is good.

Compare this to living in a place filled with compromises. Mixed messages are broadcast instead. You're a person who settles. You can't always get what you want. You need to save money. Now, do you think it makes a difference which environment you live in day after day? You bet it does.

When I walk around my home and feel those good feelings, it's very motivating. My life feels very abundant. I feel more creative. I'm more motivated to make a contribution. When I feel that the universe is supporting me so lovingly, I feel naturally inclined to give back. The old way was more stressful. My home would feel comfortable but lacking. Instead of enjoying what I had, I secretly wished I could replace it with something better. There was this nagging feeling of incompleteness.

This experience has made me more understanding of why so many highly successful people have lavishly decorated homes and offices. They're simply creating and experiencing what they desire — no compromises. When they get what they want, it helps them enjoy a more abundant state of being, whereby they can be more resourceful and creative. On the other hand, if you live and work in an environment that doesn't match what you really want, you're sending yourself a different message. You're proclaiming that life is limited and that you're powerless to fulfill your desires. You're settling for something you don't really want. Is that going to lead to happiness? No, you'll always fall short.

Releasing your blocks to abundance
Does it ever bug you that people who live in the lap of luxury are capable of much greater generosity than you are? This used to bug me a lot. How does it feel knowing that such people can donate millions (sometimes billions) of dollars to charity without sacrificing anything they truly desire?
Can you do that? Do you know for a fact that such people would have achieved this same level of giving if they denied more of their desires? Do you ever claim they should do without certain luxuries so they can give even more?

Did you ever consider that this type of thinking could be a symptom of your own lack of abundance? Have you ever thought that the ability to give so much may be a result of getting past self-denial and compromise? Is it possible to fulfill all your personal desires and become super-generous at the same time — no compromising? Is it possible that either-or thinking might be sabotaging you from achieving either of these goals?

Desire is a very personal thing. Be careful not to compare yourself to others. Bill Gates may desire a $40 million mansion, while Warren Buffet is just fine living in a modest home. Obviously they can both easily afford any kind of home on the planet, but their desires are different.

I suppose the big question you might have is, how can I possibly afford to get what I want? What if what you want costs a lot more than what you have available to spend?

I'm not suggesting that you go into debt and live beyond your means. Here's what I do recommend:

Make fewer purchases for starters. When you do make a key purchase, be willing to spend whatever it takes to get what you really want. Buy less stuff, but go for top quality.

Raise your standards for each individual purchase. Ask yourself, "What would I buy if money were no object? What would I buy if I could easily afford anything? What do I actually want, regardless of price?"

Get clear about your true desires. Forget about the price tags for a moment. Admit to yourself what you really want. Stay in that higher vibration of fulfillment and abundance, and stay out of the lower vibration of compromise and scarcity.

Instead of buying three items that are compromises, pool your resources to buy one item that you truly want, and do without the other two items for a while… at least until you can afford what you really want there as well.

Suppose you want to buy a new cell phone. Which phone and plan would you select if you won a contest that guaranteed you any phone you wanted with a lifetime plan of your choice for free?

When you're thinking about making a purchase, forget about the money at first. Don't try to determine value in terms of features vs. price. Instead, see if you can identify the very best item in accordance with your desires. If you could snap your fingers and have any item you desire for free, what would it be? Sometimes you'll pick one of the most expensive items on the market, but other times the item that best fulfills your desires will be a simpler, less expensive model.

Once you've identified what you really want, then take note of the price. If you can easily afford it, go ahead and buy it. It's what you want after all. Don't block yourself. Don't be a cheapskate. What do you think money is for anyway? Do you think you'll get more joy out of life by staring at your bank balance?

If affording the desired item seems like it would be a financial challenge, then ask yourself, "How can I afford this?" Is it really out of your league, or is it possible that you could earn it? If you come up with a way to intelligently afford the item, then make it so. Don't hold yourself back.

Could you afford the item by having a garage sale to get rid of some of your old junk? Could you put in a few more hours at work? Could you pounce on an opportunity that you've been dismissing? Could you come up with a way to create and deliver more value, thereby boosting your income? Could you acquire the item creatively, such as by bartering for it.

Do NOT obsess over the price of the item. Do NOT worry about whether or not it's a good value relative to your income. Obsess over your desire instead. Hold the intention to acquire the item with ease. Imagine that it's already yours. Picture yourself enjoying it. Feel grateful for it in advance. Think about how much you'll appreciate it.

If you do this right and avoid blocking yourself, you'll find that something rather amazing happens. The money you need may simply show up in your life. A new opportunity may present itself that makes it easy to get the money. The item itself may come into your life through an expected turn of events. The item may go on sale, making it affordable for you.

Be watchful for synchronicities related to the item. Follow them.

Desire acts like a magnet. Once you tune into your desires, allow your desires to manifest. Don't block yourself by returning to thoughts of scarcity. Don't assume you can't have what you want. Don't think about settling for a less desirable substitute. Know that what you want is already coming to you.

As far as the universe is concerned, there's no difference between a $10 item and a $10,000 item. The reason the $10K item seems more difficult to manifest is because of your beliefs. You believe it's harder to manifest, and so it is.

Start small

Begin with purchases that cause you to stretch a little but which you can easily afford. Start with purchases that aren't going to make a major dent in your finances.

When you go out to eat, order what you really want, regardless of price. If you want an appetizer, drinks, and dessert with your meal, get them. Get used to ordering off a menu without even looking at the prices.

When you go grocery shopping, buy what you actually want, even if it raises your bill a little. Stock your kitchen with the healthiest, tastiest foods you can find. Buy less food if you have to, but don't settle for cheap junk just to save a few dollars. If you go cheap, you'll likely be eating lots of wheat-, corn-, and soy-based products with different flavorings added.

Avoid phony foods that add natural flavors, artificial flavors, sugars, salt, and coloring to make them look and taste better than the mush they're really made from. Cheap foods create the illusion of variety, fooling you into eating a very limited and unhealthy diet. Spend more on fresh, organic produce to get real variety. Which items would you buy if you had a pre-paid shopping spree?

Cheap items are cheap for a reason. Quality has been sacrificed to lower the costs, and creative packaging makes it look more valuable than it really is. For example, if you buy regular white vinegar off the shelf in a grocery store (the cheapest vinegar you can get), be aware that you're buying a product that's actually made from a coal tar derivative. Use it to clean your house, but don't put that stuff in your body if you have a modicum of intelligence. The same goes for buying cheap products that include "vinegar" on the label such as the cheap name-brand ketchups and salad dressings. Buy only real food. If you can't afford to buy real food, grow it yourself for pennies on the dollar.

When buying clothes, go for quality over quantity. Get outfits that are durable, that fit you, and that look good on you, even if you have to pay more for them. If you go cheap, you'll pay for it in the long run. If you've never shopped for top quality before, it may feel uncomfortable at first. Stick with it. It gets easier over time. As you gain comfort with small purchases, up the ante a bit. Keep progressing to bigger items. Gradually condition yourself to believe that you can afford anything you want.

Appreciation and gratitude

When you get what you want, receive it with gratitude. Take time to appreciate it. Enjoy it fully. Give yourself the message that you can have whatever you desire. You just have to identify it and claim it.

This is how to live in harmony with abundance.

ATTRACT MONEY NOW!

A lot of people have one dream or the other, or they have one project or the other that they wish they had money to finance. A lot of people complain about not having enough money for this, and not enough money for that. I do not think money should ever be the issue. If you understand how the law of attraction works, you would know that money should not be the issue as long as you have a solid definite purpose for that money in your mind.

When I learnt about the law of attraction for the first time although I had been reading books and articles relating to the principle, but didn't know what it was called, I was so excited about it that I wrote a book and published it all within 3 months of my reading the book titled, THE SECRET. I didn't have a dime in the account, and I still do not know how I did it. For evidence, go to Amazon.com and kindles, you would find my books there. But what I further learnt was that I had been in the possession of the secret law of attraction for a long time. I had been using it unconsciously for a long time, but the book just opened my eyes to a better understanding of it. My own book, which I wrote under 2 weeks and I published within 2 months, is based solely on attracting money into one's life using the law, but the law of attraction can be used to attract anything into one's life. Anything like a good relationship, happiness, a good job.

Incase you do not know about the law of attraction, it is one of the 11 universal laws that states that- you attract to yourself your most prominent thoughts. That means, what you think about, you bring about. It sounds too simple right? But that is a fact, and the problem is that a lot of us think so little of ourselves, and we end up getting the physical materialization of our thoughts on the outside. Christians are meant to be Christ-like right? Why do so many think so little of themselves when Christ said- if ye have faith as little as a mustard seed, you would say to the mountain, move to yonder place, and it shall be so, why do people still have poverty consciousness, when as human beings we have been blessed with God powers?

I would like to briefly talk about attracting any amount of money you want to yourself. The first thing you need to do is to have a definite purpose for that money in your mind- what you want to use the money for should be imprinted in your mind. Then, you have to believe and have faith that you can get that money. You do not have to care where the money would come from; don't worry; the Father within you would handle that.

Just think of what you want to use the money for, and see yourself already in possession of that thing, or enjoying whatever it is you want to use the money for. Every morning when you awake, and every night before you go to bed, visualize your desire as already a reality. I assure you that if you do this continuously for 2 weeks, you would get any amount you wish for.

BECOMING AN ENLIGHTENED MILLIONAIRE.

If we are Pure Potentiality, can we do anything right? The answer is yes, but there's always a price to pay to whatever we create.

As conscious, intentional creators, our work is to accept our unlimitedness. Our first and foremost goal is to fully comprehend that we are Divine, unlimited children of God. Thus, the heart of your question: If we are unlimited and pure potentiality then anything is possible, correct? YES!

At the core of our being we and the Father (the Divine Creator, the life force that creates worlds, God) are one. We absolutely have the power and the capacity to turn water into wine, grow new limbs and organs, walk on water, and even 'win the lottery'. However, remember the story of King Midas. He loved wealth and gold so much that when he was granted one wish, he wished that everything he touched would turn to gold.

Shortly, everything he loved, his wife and children, his servants, his beloved horse, even his clothes were turned to gold, exactly what he said he wanted. As the fable's moral depicts, "Be careful what you go asking for." When we are truly aligned with the essence of our being (our unlimitedness), we are aligned with integritous, harmonious, life-supporting and benign actions and outcomes.

It is not possible to be in alignment with our pure-potentiality and sell something that no one wants. The two are simply not congruent. Just like it's not possible to be in alignment with the nature of our divinity and commit murder. The two are simply not in vibrational harmony. Think of those who become millionaires in an unethical manner. They manifested their 'millionaire status'; therefore they must have had a prosperity consciousness. In the end, however, there's always a price to pay for misaligned actions.

Did you hear about the "millionaire spammers"? Jeremy Jaynes and Jessica DeGroot were making in excess of $900,000.00 a month sending unsolicited email. Not a bad income. However, they were then sentenced to 9 years in prison because of 'how' they made their money.

There's always a cause and an effect. There's always a price and a profit for every action and decision we make. On the other hand, aligned actions may not always appear to be inspired by a 'sure-thing-idea'. They are, however, inspired from a place of higher consciousness. Millions of self-made millionaires amassed their fortunes on ideas that everyone else thought were crazy. Do you remember those slimy, crawling, plastic octopi also known as wacky wall walkers of the 80's? Can you believe that nearly $100 million was made on these silly, sticky, gooey, octopi that children threw against the wall and our ceilings? In fact, I bet some of us still have the slime trail from where they crawled down our walls!

And, who would have thought that millions and millions of those silicone bracelets (Lance Armstrong's Live Strong, the Leukemia Society, etc.) have been sold? If the inventor had asked a fashion expert if it was a million dollar idea, the response would have been, "Are you nuts?"

Even though the pair of million dollar ideas above were not obvious winners, the inventors followed their guidance, took enough aligned action, and the delivery and fulfillment of the 'ideas' were congruent and harmonious with the essence of our divine nature; the essence of a higher consciousness.

The formula for an enlightened millionaire in a nutshell.
1. Align your beliefs with the essence of your pure potentiality.
2. Ask for, listen to, and actively follow Divine Guidance.
3. Take consistent, enlightened, faithful, and bold actions.
4. Be willing to fail (because you cannot) and be willing to begin again (because you are never really beginning again).
5. Be grateful for every step of the way, all the while maintaining your absolute faith and certainty in the obtainment of your dream.

Start over with number 1 above every day!

In the pursuit of enlightened wealth, the path is the purpose more than the destination. And, as unlimited beings Divine Wealth is our Birthright!

MONEY AND SPIRITUALITY

Money and Spirituality - do they mix?

The hoary argument that you cannot have both - spirituality and abundance continues to proliferate and entangle the minds and experience of many seekers. As a culture, we constantly deal with the subconscious remnants caused by the conflict between money and spirituality. We have allowed toxic ideas to pervade our unlimited essence like a virus destroying our intrinsic right to wealth and fulfillment.

Ideas such as 'money is the root of all evil', that 'it's easier to get a camel through the eye of a needle than for a rich man to get into heaven', and that 'if you are rich, then you must be either a crook, selfish, or hardened' abound in the global consciousness poisoning our natural right to wealth.

Additionally, the infamous subconscious impression amongst many spiritual practitioners and seekers; you cannot be spiritual and a servant of the Divine, if you charge for your talent or knowledge continues to be the self-imposed prison that forces many spiritual workers to thrash about in a sea of lack.

These are just an infinitesimal sampling of the money-and- spirituality-don't-mix disease.

Indeed, if one becomes consumed with the pursuit of wealth from the external vantage point, their spiritual unification will be compromised. They may achieve wealth but at the cost of the fulfillment of their divine destiny and at the expense of personal peace. On the other side, when one pursues spirituality as their premiere directive, there is a point at which they will meet a fork in the road. They will be met with the decision to remain singularly dedicated to their personal, individual, self-seeking spiritual pursuits or expand into a place of connection with the greater spiritual community. There's nothing wrong with either approach.

However, there is a level of responsibility that is arguably unfulfilled. When one's personal spiritual pursuits yield individual impact and neglects or bypasses the conscientious responsibility of how their personal peace could impact their community or their world; the question of individual self-absorbed importance versus planetary importance remains.

For this reason, it is my belief that it is indeed my responsibility to fulfill a level of prosperity that affords me the capacity to participate and influence the greatest amount of change.

If you were to ask any of the premiere spiritual and evolutionary entrepreneurs, healers, philosophers, and social artists of our time how they feel about money and spirituality, they would agree that the more prosperous a social artist is the more impact they can facilitate.

Mother Theresa renounced her worldly possessions. However, at the same time, she knew the power of prosperity when aligned with an enlightened altruistic cause. She attracted all the resources and financial contributions necessary to support, feed, and spiritually heal millions. She did not do this by rejecting prosperity or by condemning those who seek it, but by unifying the Truth of her being as pure potential and therefore both spiritual and rich.

It's true, there is a fine balance. When one pursuit or the other becomes our primary focus, we are not in alignment with our greatest human potential. Additionally, the law of psychological reciprocity demands that we give in order to receive. There will be no harvest without a period of prepping, planting, and fertilizing.

I believe that this incredible time on the planet is one of profound transformational and evolutionary change. I believe that we are light workers creating a planetary society built on the principles of spiritual peace and universal love. Therefore, I gratefully embrace that with prosperity I am a force to be reckoned with. Without prosperity, I can only inspire change at the level of consciousness that causes my own lack.

The Kabbalah, in my limited studies, has had a profound impact on my understanding of the Universal Laws. One such transformational idea that has supported my integral understanding of the law of psychological reciprocity is the concept of "the bread of shame".

When we get something for nothing, there is a part of our being that rejects this hand-out. We spiritually and intuitively regret the free offering because we didn't earn or rightfully deserve it. Additionally, we are not spiritually or physically prepared to manage the offering. If you've ever played a sport, then imagine how nonplussed it would feel to win the game as a result of the other team sitting down on the field just so you could win.

Is this a victory that you'd be excited about? NO! It's a terribly disappointing victory! A no-effort victory yields no emotional or celebratory excitement. If there's no competition - why play the game?

Think also about the troubling statistics of lottery winners and what evidence this supports in relationship to the bread of shame. "The reality is that 70 percent of all lottery winners will squander away their winnings in a few years," the Connecticut financial advisers Michael Begin and Darl LePage said in a news release. "In the process, they will see family and friendships destroyed and the financial security they hoped for disappear.

Statistics show lottery winners often go bankrupt, get divorced and have family feuds; winning the lottery isn't always a dream.

I have given thousands upon thousands of dollars worth of complimentary coaching and courses to students in need. Unfortunately, no matter how much I give away, I'm most often disappointed in the student's inability to use the information. When it's free there's no skin-in-the-game! When a person doesn't have any pulling desire to hold themselves accountable, because it didn't cost them anything to participate, the motivation to actually apply the information is simply not there.

I have been shunned and berated by spiritual seekers not understanding the law of abundance and the law of psychological reciprocity. They want to know how ethical it is for someone to make a living or worse 'get rich' by selling information.

The truth is that everything I teach is readily available for free. This is also true for any teacher on the planet. If one wants to know what a teacher knows, all they have to do is their homework and research to find it. One never has to pay for knowledge if they are willing to do the work. However, just as the bread of shame principle prevents us from rejoicing in an undeserving victory, when we receive the key to free knowledge we seldom, if ever, use it to open the door.

Therefore, I beseech every spiritual worker to honor and acknowledge their Divine inheritance. Step up to the truth that you were born to be unlimited and financially prosperous.

The next time the idea that spirituality doesn't include prosperity crosses your mind, rebuke the idea! Instead, embrace a higher calling to accept your unlimitedness, embrace not only your Divine Right to financial peace but your inherent responsibility to be prosperous. The more you have, whether it's financial abundance or mental, emotional, or physical abundance, the more profound an impact you may facilitate. You owe it to yourself and your fellow light-workers to be prosperous in all ways.

Here's an exercise for you! If you notice any idea within this book is creating a negative response within, then take your inkling to your journal right away. Write down any thought that may be causing you resistance or any thought that suggests you can't have both money and spirituality.

Until one is aware of their limitations, they will be bound by them. Once you have your limiting beliefs on paper, firmly deny it. Emphatically refuse to tolerate anything that keeps you and your Divine Right to prosperity separate. Affirm the opposite of any limiting belief, now.

If you know EFT (Emotional Freedom Technique) then use it now to get rid of any and all negative thoughts about spirituality and money. Use any releasing method that you know to eliminate any and all resentments about people making money in the spiritual market, people making money in general, wanting to get something for nothing, or you earning a living as a light-worker.

Start with yourself; acknowledge any limiting baggage that no longer serves you and be willing to renew your consciousness with the knowledge that Divine prosperity is your birthright. Allow your inner being to remind you - Abundance is everywhere! There's more than enough to go around! Claim yours now.

HOW TO MANIFEST MONEY FAST USING THE LAW OF ATTRACTION AND EMOTIONAL FREEDOM TECHNIQUE (EFT)

How do I Manifest Money Immediately? I need to manifest a lot of money fast - What can I do to attract money now?

Use Emotional Freedom Technique (EFT) to apply the Law of Detachment, first! For most of us, whenever we have to manifest something immediately, we almost automatically become anxious, fearful and doubtful.

If you have to manifest something immediately then you are dancing with one foot nailed to the floor! The nail that makes you spin is attachment; the attachment is the 'fear that immediately isn't fast enough.' Since what we put our attention upon expands, the fear actually attracts the opposite of a solution. If we are afraid of 'not getting the money' then we don't get the money. If we are afraid of 'not having a safe home' then we get not having a safe home.

It's important that we recognize our fearful and doubtful thoughts and engage the law of detachment. The law of detachment is the act of employing absolute certainty and pure faith in the belief that our desire is certain and already within our reach.

With the law of attraction and emotional freedom technique (EFT), we can both harness the quantum power of the energy that creates worlds (our positive thoughts) and eliminate the emotional impediments (our negative thoughts/emotions) that block what we really want from manifesting. In other words, EFT allows us to apply the law of detachment with sincere consistency. With EFT we neutralize our negative emotions and limiting beliefs. When we are neutral with our fears then the dreams and visions that we've been sending out to the Universe for years can finally have a safe landing; we can finally prepare the runway to be clear of debris so that our flight can land safely and prosperously.

Think of EFT as the can-opener for your dreams. Before the fabulous invention of the hand-held can-opener, breaching a can of green beans required lots of effort, concentration, a steady hand and a sharp knife. You would eventually get to the food, but it would require a great deal of forced effort. Cutting and prying off the metal top ensured that you'd be plenty hungry by the time you enjoyed your first bite of sodium-packed vegetables.

Without intentional creation, most of us live our lives with a great deal of forced effort. And, by the time we 'get the money, the home, the job, the relationship' we are absolutely ravenous; not to mention exhausted and fearful of having to 'do it all over again tomorrow.'

By using EFT along with your creative visualization and manifesting exercises you have the ability to set free the positive vibes that have been vacuum sealed inside of you; you set free the potent imaginings that allow you to accept your divinity and harness your Divine powers of creation. If you are not manifesting what you want fast enough, use EFT to get rid of the doubts and you're guaranteed to be happier. When you release the negative beliefs, if what you believe you want is in alignment with what you really want most right now, then you can't help but have it materialize.

How do you use Emotional Freedom Technique (EFT) with the Law of Attraction?

Using the situation, "I need to manifest money fast", we can only assume that there's a reason that 'fast' is important. Therefore, let's assume that something bad might happen if you don't get the money fast. So when you want to use EFT to employ the law of detachment, figure out what you're attached to; continue to probe your thoughts until you identify what you're afraid of and what negative beliefs cause you distress. With the desire "How do I manifest money fast?" you can uncover your specific fears by asking yourself "fear- prompting" questions. For example; if I don't manifest enough money, what's the worst thing that I'm afraid of will happen? If I never get the money I need, what will happen? If I can't work hard enough what will happen? If I can't borrow the money what will happen? If I don't find a way to get the money, what is the worst thing that this says about me? If I don't find a way to get the money, what does this remind me of? If I don't manifest the money quickly, what will others say about me?

As law of attraction students, we've been taught NOT to look at the negative. However, with EFT, we want to acknowledge and shine the spotlight on anything that may be subconsciously sabotaging our positive vibes.

Don't worry - we won't be "attracting" by acknowledging our limiting beliefs but instead we'll be releasing them from our vibration once and for all. All you want to do is use EFT on those negative thoughts in order to sweep clean your attractor beacon. This is the ONE time you WANT to acknowledge your fears and doubts in order to release them from your creative vibration.

Therefore, identify the negative and hurtful thoughts that cause you pain and use these thoughts to form the set-up phrases with EFT.

Again using the "manifest money fast" example, the set-up phrases that would allow you to use the power of EFT to get in there and rip the limiting beliefs out of your system and replace them with a sense of emotional neutrality might be:

1. Even though I'm afraid that I don't have the ability to manifest enough money fast enough, I deeply and completely love and accept myself.

   Reminder phrase: I can't make enough money fast enough.

2. Even though I'm afraid that I'll lose my home if I don't manifest the money fast enough, what if I could make peace with what is? Reminder phrase: I'll lose my home.

3. Even though I'm terrified of being enslaved to my financial impotence for the rest of my life, I deeply and completely love and accept myself!
Reminder phrase: I'm a financial failure.

4. Even though I don't know how to get enough money fast enough and feel like it's a futile desire, what if I was capable of accomplishing anything?
Reminder phrase: I don't know how to make enough money fast enough.

5. Even though I doubt I will ever have the money I need to live the way I want to, I deeply and completely love, accept, and appreciate myself.
Reminder phrase: This shame and doubt.

The really great news is that you can be releasing your limiting beliefs in less than one hour from now, even if this is the first time you've ever heard of EFT! By expanding your moments of peace, you're automatically enacting the law of detachment. You cannot feel attached and at peace at the same time. You can, however, feel attached and apathetic or sad at the same time. Your benchmark is neutrality. If you do not reach a level of ZERO emotion or a state of neutrality, then you've not cleared the limiting beliefs completely.

You want to be persistent with conquering your fears, limiting emotions, and doubts using this EFT process until you've wiped out all negative emotions. It may take 30 minutes or it may take 30 days but if you want to finally experience a break-through with your manifesting skills then begin using EFT to enact the Law of Detachment, even if it's just 3 minutes a day.

IS THINKING ENOUGH IN MANIFESTING MONEY?

To manifest money successfully using the Law of Attraction you want to "think" a completely different way than most people tell you to think when trying to manifest money using the Law of Attraction. Just "thinking about attraction" by doing money affirmations or other abundance and prosperity affirmations isn't enough and this chapter will expose to you the why and what to do about it.

When most people start experimenting with the Law of Attraction, it's usually to manifest money, although sometimes people will start out trying to manifest better health or better relationships. But, the fact remains that manifesting money is usually the primary goal for newcomers when starting out using the Law of Attraction.

The funny thing about this is these newcomers usually have great need when it comes to needing money; so their "energetic signature" is need, yet they usually place great expectations on the Law of Attraction to deliver magical results. When the magical results don't occur after spending a short time to learn how to manifest money, the traditional "intellectual" way by doing money affirmations or repeating money mantras or perhaps repeating one specific wealth affirmation, then most people get disillusioned and blame the Law of Attraction for not working.

Although this is typical for most people, it does not have to be their only choice because new techniques and practices around changing our "energetic signature" have been proven successful and replace the outdated "thinking only mode" of doing money affirmations, abundance and prosperity affirmations, and abundance wealth affirmations and gives people hope to manifest money successfully with the Law of Attraction.

One of the newest finds in the study of using the Law of Attraction is "working energetically" instead of "thinking intellectually." What this means is to stop relying on just your mind, and to start relying on your entire physical body to feel the energy of what you're trying to attract. So, how do you do this? It's actually rather simple when you know a few tricks. One of the tricks is to change your subconscious "homing pigeon" part of your brain to send out the "energetic signal" that having money is good.

While this sounds simple, most people miss this point altogether when trying to manifest money using the Law of Attraction.
Most people go for getting the result of having lots of money, but disregard all the negative subconscious beliefs they have inside themselves surrounding money. These negative subconscious beliefs then send out a conflicting "energetic signature" to the Law of Attraction that negates most of the effort people put into doing their money affirmations, abundance and prosperity affirmations or continually repeating money mantras or even one specific wealth affirmation.

One way of releasing these negative subconscious beliefs around money is to use silent subliminal meditations that target many of the negative beliefs we have picked up from our "poverty minded" society. These types of meditations are uncommon, however, since this particular technique is cutting-edge on how to use the Law of Attraction to manifest money.

Another one of the new tricks is to "tune your physical body" to the vibration of what you want to attract. This has been proven to be a much stronger technique than just reciting money affirmations. Once you learn how to manifest money by doing energetic exercises that teach your body how to feel the vibration of what you want to attract, you can successfully manifest money or anything else you want with the Law of Attraction.

Learning how to manifest money with the Law of Attraction by learning some of these latest, cutting-edge techniques that practically force the Law of Attraction to work give you deeper, more concrete ways to manifest money because you've removed your subconscious blocks to receiving money, as well as have enlisted the help of your entire physical body to attract money instead of just relying on your mind alone to be strong enough to manifest what you desire.

These techniques of changing your subconscious mind through silent subliminals and learning energetic exercises that tune your body to match what you desire are much more effective and easier than simply reciting money affirmations because these new techniques work on much deeper energetic levels than you can attain through reciting affirmations or other approaches that only center around using "conscious thinking processes."

TEN STRATEGIES TO CREATING LAVISH PROSPERITY

I would like to drive home this point that your point of attraction is right now and the Universe does not know the difference between real and imagined; it simply responds to your vibration in the moment. Therefore, fantasize, visualize and day-dream your reality!

Here are the 10 creating lavish prosperity strategies:

1. Spend Freely Mentally -- Everywhere you go, say to yourself, "I have the financial ability to purchase anything I desire in cash right now; therefore what do I want, right now? I shall have one of these and two of those and I'll have my assistant pick them up for me this afternoon." Put a 100-dollar bill in your wallet and spend it 50 times throughout the day. See it and multiply it by 10 every time you open your wallet.

2. Create a Gratitude Journal: Log and give thanks for all the abundance you have now and have always had every morning and every evening.

3. Release the Old: Create a vacuum! Clean out your closet, get rid of the clutter, use your good stationery, and wear your most expensive perfume!

4. Show God you know his promise will be kept and exhaust the resources at hand, pay the bills you can now, know the Divine is your source and your supply is inexhaustible!

5. Play the million dollars a month game. If you had to spend a million dollars every month for 6 months, what would you buy, how would you tithe, how would you feel and what would you do? Really go through the motions of what you would have to do to spend that money!

6. Forgive yourself for your debts and forgive your debtors! Release anyone that owes you anything and caste your burden of debts on the Christ within. Give it to God!

7. Create Abundance Affirmations and reminders and place them everywhere.

   a. I love being debt free and I enjoy purchasing anything I desire in cash, when I desire it!

b. I love driving my new _____, I feel so free and fabulous in my new ride!

c. My income far exceeds all of my wants, needs and desires!

d. I rejoice in my abundant prosperity and financial freedom!

e. I love giving and receiving freely!

f. I am rich, rich, rich and I love it!

g. Abundance is my birthright and I now command $500,000,000.00 into my account now! Times 10!

8. Script a vision of how you will have to adjust your life to your new abundant lifestyle. How will you make the changes, what preparations need to be made, how will it look, feel, taste, smell? Walk in this new vision and elaborate and expand it everyday!

9. Become superstitiously silly about the riches that are coming your way and associate every day activities to the energy of more money. For example, every time you shift into drive say, "I'm driving into abundance now!" Every time you find a penny, pick it up, giving thanks for the hundreds of thousands more that are coming your way. Every time you receive and/or pay a bill say, "I give thanks for your complete payment and for every dollar I release, ten more comes my way." Every time you pass a beggar, give to them and bless them for helping you know your supply is endless and immediate!

10. Create a Prosperity Collage! Cut out magazine clippings, newspaper ads of items you want, words that inspire you and imagine, visualize and fantasize with your collage every day.

TITHING: HOW AND WHERE TO DO IT TO ACTIVATE THE LAW OF TEN-FOLD RETURN

Is there such a thing as over-giving or misguided giving? The reason I ask is because throughout my growing up years, all I remember of my mother is that she gives to everyone, and she is grossly taken advantage of. My mother is a wonderful woman who did not know how to say no to individuals who took gross advantage of her kindness. I had to do a lot of forgiveness work during the last few years, when it became so clear how much everyone took from my mother and no one was really there to care for her but me. Truly, it has been a challenge for me being on the spiritual path and doing the best I can to continue to love, give, serve and forgive and witness individuals coming to me like perpetual charity cases.

When our giving is out of balance, we can be stripped of a healthy sense of reciprocity and honoring boundaries. If you are giving too much then it can absolutely create a negative attractor pattern. When our giving leaves us feeling used, taken advantage of, and even abused, we must take a step back to re-assess our giving intentions. If our giving is coming from a place of healthy generosity with no strings attached, then we are in alignment with healthy tithing.

However, if our giving intention is from a place of obligation, guilt, shame, a need to control, a need to make restitution for a wrong-doing, or a need to feel or be acknowledged as a certain type of person; a need to be thought of as generous, powerful, or successful, for example, then this intention is out-of-balance and therefore our giving is out of balance.

Over-giving comes from a co-dependent need to be validated and cherished, which is always inspired by a lack of self-confidence and an inability to be our own source of happiness. When we give to make up for our inadequacy, we will never be able to give enough to fill the void we feel inside. The solution is the same as it is for any other ill-belief - to work towards pure self-confidence; to work towards fully embracing an absolute certainty of your unlimitedness; a belief and firm knowingness that you are indeed a Divine Child of God, worthy of all that you desire. From this place, you'll be inspired to give according to the higher order of life and not from a place of limitation.

I would want to state that there's a difference between a donation and a tithe. The two have different intentions and therefore different attractor patterns. When we donate to a cause, we are attached to the outcome. We are saying, "I believe in how this money will be spent and therefore I will give to you." This attachment diminishes the vibration and therefore isn't giving in the pure sense of the intention: to acknowledge God, the big-U (Universe), as the source and supply of all our good.

When we tithe to some source where we feel spiritually nourished, we are not giving in order to receive something in return. We are giving in acknowledgment only of a sense of spiritual fulfillment and a desire to simply honor God (the-All-that-is). We give with the pure intent of not being attached to how the money is used but we give in order to share, to spread the wealth, and to acknowledge the abundant, opulent, all-providing promise of our Divine Inheritance.

Both a donation and a tithe are positive and fabulous ways to share your wealth and increase your prosperity consciousness. However, anytime there is attachment, there are diminished positive returns. Detached tithing alone from your first fruits with the only intent being to show God you believe in abundance; to show God you know that the Divine within is your only source and supply is the only giving/tithing/spiritual act that initiates the Law of Ten-Fold Return.

My suggestion is to keep giving as you feel comfortable, for right now. Then, work towards tithing 10% without attachment to how the money will be used to some source where you feel spiritually fed while continuing to support causes that you believe in with additional funds.

Can't find a place where you feel spiritually fed? Look harder, it may be the little old lady on the corner that smiles everyday when you pass, it may be the author of that 200 word book that changed how you parent your children, or it may be the workshop assistant leader that shared her experience so boldly, or it may be your spiritual center, and it may even be a charitable organization provided you make a distinction between where I'm spiritually fed and when I want this money to do a certain thing.

Choose to give anonymously if necessary, in order to give freely without any attachment to the outcome. God will always return what you give and then some. Think about it - Who can out-give God? Listen to this question; if what I've given does not add up to 10%, does that mean I haven't given/tithe enough? I'm not presently working and am living modestly off my savings but I donate some money to my chosen charities twice a year and I give via helping out as a volunteer, etc. Isn't it really about giving/sharing whatever with good intentions rather than it being about a fixed percentage?

Answer: Yes, it is about giving and sharing from a positive intention place. However, there is a law that has been set in motion for thousands of years now. The Law of Ten-Fold Return works whether we realize it or not on the 10% of our first fruits equation.

The Universe will return to us in the same manner and perspective that we give from. There's no need to judge anything that you've done up until now as not good enough. However, you may want to look at the fear around giving 10%. If you fear that you won't have enough, then you are keeping yourself in poverty consciousness. Deal with the fear by expanding your willingness to trust in the Divine; by acknowledging your only source and supply is the big-U, God, the omnipotent Presence that is the sole provider of all things in your life.

Meditate and pray on expanding your ability to accept your inheritance and ask for guidance on how to 'throw open the windows of heaven' by tithing the full 10%. For anyone who is feeling reticent about tithing 10%, try starting where you are and proceed from there.

When I was a starving business owner in college and full of poverty consciousness, I didn't feel like I had any extra money to give. However, I also knew that it felt really bad not to help the people who were worse off than me. I used to keep apples in my purse to give away. This was my way, at the time, of increasing my giving consciousness. As I look back, I see that I went from apples, to coupons and other food items, to quarters, to dollars, to self-help tapes and books, to giving 10% of my unexpected income, to tithing after my bills were paid, to now tithing from my first fruits, 10% of my net income which is the optimal goal. If you are a solo-entrepreneur, it's 10% of your gross income before your personal expenses but after realistic, required business expenses.

If you can make the jump to tithe 10% of your unexpected income, this will be a great eye-opener about the rewards of tithing. Set yourself a goal to give 10% of any monies that you receive from unexpected sources including any unexpected savings that you receive. Keep a log and give 10% of that amount weekly.

Record your thoughts, feelings and observations and try to give more each month until you are truly acknowledging your abundance by giving 10% of your first fruits every month. Prosperity is your birthright. Accept it and claim it.

Take this for the essence of what it means:

"Bring all the tithes into the storehouse, that there may be food in my house, and prove me now by it, says the Lord of hosts, if I will not open the windows of Heaven for you and pour you out a blessing, that there shall not be room enough to receive it." - Malachi 3:10

If you are an EFT'er: It may help to clear some negative association by doing some EFT (emotional freedom technique) with phrases such as:

1. Even though I feel nauseous when I think about the church taking our money
2. Even though I despise tithing because of the hypocritical association it brings up between the church and my childhood
3. Even though I associate giving and tithing with church and that makes me feel mistreated and dis-empowered

Then try positive implanting statements such as:

1. Never the less, I choose to release any limiting thoughts about giving now.
2. Never the less, I choose to give freely from the heart.
3. Never the less, I choose to honor my Divine Inheritance and fully acknowledge God as my only source and supply through giving and tithing freely.
4. Never the less, I choose to be joy-filled and empowered by tithing 10% of my first fruits freely to wherever I am spiritual fed.

Planning to give will increase your experience of the joy that comes from regular tithing. Additionally, any time you increase your joy, you increase your vibrational frequency which in turn adds positive attraction and magnetism to all of your other goals as well.

HOW TO USE EFT TO GIVE AND GET MORE

When you want to receive, don't get caught making the common mistake of not giving or even thinking that you cannot GIVE! When you want to achieve, don't get caught making the common mistake of not taking action or even thinking that you cannot ACT now!

The Law of Reciprocity and the Law of Giving decree that you get what you give.

Giving, however, is not just about giving money or about giving to others. Giving includes giving time, talent, treasures, love, support, understanding, patience, and giving through physical and emotional support (action) to yourself as well as to others.

The definition of "Give" includes hundreds of ways that the action of "giving" is fulfilled, including:
1. to bring forth or to bear
2. to yield or produce
3. to furnish or contribute
4. to proffer to another
5. to be a source of
6. to make gifts or donations

In order to receive, you must give; in order to achieve, you must take action.

There is a reciprocal action that occurs with every action you take. When you hear spiritual teachers say that giving and receiving are the same, it's because the Universe must create balance and as you give, you shall receive. For every action you take there is an equal or greater reaction that must be returned to you. For every thought you submit, the balance sheet is adjusted and the Universe must return like energy into your life.

Sir Isaac Newton captured the essence of natural balance when he codified the law of physics which states every action precipitates a reciprocal event - an equal and opposite reaction. It is not by mere coincidence that mathematics - the language of science - encodes logic into a device called an equation which requires its elements to be equivalent on opposite sides of the argument. From simple addition to quantum mechanics, reciprocal balance is a prevailing dynamic which even the rules of cause and effect must obey.

Recently, my uncle's children were in the backseat and a beggar at a stoplight held a sign that read, "Anything helps!" Usually, I rumble around looking for something to give. Sometimes, it's cash, sometimes it's food, and sometimes it's brand-new self-help audio programs, books, etc. However, on this day, I was in a hurry and I must have just not felt like giving. When Parker and Ashlyn realized that I wasn't going to give to him, they both screamed, "but uncle you said, NEVER PASS UP AN OPPORTUNITY TO GIVE!"

The light turned green and I went through the light without giving. However, the incessant rumbling coming from the kids combined with my own inner commitments simply required me to do a double U-turn in order to give to this man immediately!

 Phew! That felt SOOOOO much better! It doesn't matter WHAT he did with the money - what matters is that I GAVE!!! Thank you, God, for giving me the opportunity to give!

Aligned giving does not create imbalance, lack, misuse, debt, or co-dependence. There will always be an aligned way to give that does not include the negative results of over- giving; and there will always be aligned actions that do not include the negative results of distressed actions.

What I have discovered, with my own walk of giving and with working with clients, is that we ALL have reasons to NOT give and reasons NOT to take action:
1. I don't have the time.
2. I don't have the extra money.

3. I don't think it will do that person any good.
4. I don't want to put forth the effort.
5. It will take too long to see any results from me taking that road.
6. I don't want that kind of commitment.
7. I don't want it to be hard.
8. I'm afraid there won't be enough .
9. I'm afraid that I can't make ends meet if I give it away.
10. I'm afraid that I will be more exhausted if I commit to giving my time in that way.
11. I'm afraid I'll fail if I take action on that.
12. I'm afraid that if I 'do this' then I'll be successful and success will create less freedom.
13. I'm afraid I'll be taken for granted if I give any more love to my significant other.
14. I'm afraid I'll be 'used' if I give more.
15. I'm afraid people will expect it from now on, if I start giving.
16. I'll do it later.

This is anti-prosperity consciousness. Scarcity consciousness will prevent you from giving and from courageously taking action.

If you find that you have reasons or excuses for not giving, then you can be rest assured that somewhere in your subconscious mind and your vibration is the fear that there isn't enough for you or you're not enough and therefore you can't give more. Scarcity consciousness, poverty consciousness, lack consciousness - any subconscious thought that causes you to NOT give and to NOT take action will prevent you from having the abundant and fulfilled life you desire.

Anti-prosperity consciousness actually resonates with the poverty, lack, scarcity, struggle, redundancy, effort, hardship, distress, and deprivation that you DON'T want! With EFT (Emotional Freedom Technique) you can eliminate the anti-prosperity consciousness that prevents you from joyfully, consistently and confidently practicing your unlimitedness by giving and by taking action.

Remember, every thought holds a vibrational frequency that attracts into our lives a parallel experience. EFT supports conscious creators by neutralizing the vibrational consequences of our subconscious negative thoughts and beliefs. When we neutralize the negative thoughts, we dissipate the negative vibes and the vibes that remain are the pure, positive thoughts about the life we really want!

Try the following:

1. Even though I don't have enough 'time/money/talent' to share, what if I accepted my divine potential and shared freely anyway?
2. Even though I'm afraid to give my 'money/time' away, what if I fearlessly gave freely and joyously?
3. Even though I don't want to give any more than I do, what if I looked forward to giving freely and openly?
4. Even though I'm afraid that there won't be any extra or enough, what if I allowed the Universe to support and flow abundance to me and I chose to give, now?
5. Even though I don't trust what 'they' will do with my money, what if I loved the act of giving so much that I gave freely and without attachment?
6. Even though I'm afraid to take action, I might make a mistake, what if I fearlessly and courageously took action anyway?
7. Even though I withhold and I am selfish with my time/money/talent/things; what if I could choose to give freely and openly every time?
8. Even though I procrastinate, what if I took bold action regularly and consistently, now?

Negative reminders:
1. This fear that there's not enough.
2. This fear that I'll make a mistake.
3. This fear that I can't do it perfectly.
4. This doubt that I'll ever have enough.
5. This inability to trust in the Universe.
6. This lack of belief that I'm meant to be prosperous.
7. This inability to believe that as I give, I shall receive.

8. This procrastination.
9. This fear that I'll be taken for granted/used/abused.
10. This inactivity.
11. This self-sabotage.

Positive Implants:
1. What if I openly and freely gave of my time/talent/treasures?
2. What if I loved giving freely?
3. What if I trusted in my divine inheritance?
4. What if I held absolute faith that as I give, I shall receive and then some?
5. What if I gave freely without attachment to the outcome?
6. What if I gave just because it felt good?
7. What if I allowed myself to test the law of giving and just gave from my heart fearlessly?
8. What if I trusted myself to set appropriate boundaries and still give freely?
9. What if I followed my inspired desire to give and took bold, courageous consistent action, now?
10. What if I never passed up an opportunity to give?

Remember, every time you refuse to give and every time you refuse to take inspired/aligned action is a missed opportunity to take one more step towards your goal of prosperous, joy-filled living!

Visualize what you want using creative visualization and the law of attraction but use EFT (Emotional Freedom Technique) to eliminate the limited thinking that prevents you from acting in accordance to your vision, now!
Eventually, if you take enough action and you give enough that one more step will be the victory step; that one last step will be the one at the top!

GOD'S WILL FOR OUR MONEY

My main emotions in regard to money at Bethlehem are gratitude and hope, not anxiety. God has always met our needs. I would insult God if I fretted over his timing. So, Thank you. Thank you. Thank you, for your giving. For 12 years now I have watched our merciful God meet all my needs. Thank you for your part in that mercy.

I am writing this to encourage those of you who are still struggling with how to handle your finances in relation to the church. Please think and pray about several things:

1. All your money is God's. Psalm 24:1, "The earth is the LORD's, and all it contains, The world, and those who dwell in it." You have your money and possessions and life on loan. As a trust. You are the manager of another's trust fund.

2. How we disburse God's trust fund that is, our income and inheritances should reflect his values and priorities. We will all be held accountable for managing his money according to his word. Luke 16:12, "If you have not been faithful in the use of that which is another's, who will give you that which is your own?"

3. God will see to it that you have enough to provide for your needs and for "every good work," including those appointed for your church (worship, teaching, outreach, missions, mutual care, etc). I know no stories of people who have given so generously that God did not meet their needs. 2 Corinthians 9:8, "And God is able to provide you with every blessing in abundance, so that you may always have enough of everything and may provide in abundance for every good work."

4. Expenses always expand to fill the income. This means that almost all of us "just get by" no matter what we make. This in turn means that discretionary giving which is put off to the end of the pay period will usually not happen. We won't give because we don't think we can afford it; but if you write the check to the cause of Christ first, then you will, as always, still "just get by." I encourage you to "seek the kingdom first" by writing the ministry check first (Matthew 6:33).

5. The Bible encourages both spontaneity and discipline in giving. Remember the overflowing generosity of the widow: "Out of her poverty [she] put in all that she had" (Luke 31:4). But the usual way is to give in a disciplined, regular and proportional way:

On the first day of every week each one of you is to put aside and save, as he may prosper (1 Corinthians 16:2). I urge you to build this regularity and priority into your giving. Tithing (10% of your income) is a good Biblical starting point (Matthew 23:23). Go for it. God will not let you down.

ABOUT THE AUTHOR

Joseph Dolapo Otaiku is a prolific personal development, motivational and corporate speaker and a protégé of Bob Proctor, James Allen, and Wallace D. Wattles amongst others. He is the President/CEO of RichIP Concept Limited, a company located in Nigeria but does global business and he is the founder of THE MASTER'S COLT ARENA, a foundation designed to distribute the resources attracted to all for the good of all. He was born in Lagos, Nigeria some three decades ago.

His intellectual abilities about the universal laws has really garnered lots of interest from friends and clients alike who get dazzled at his intelligence of the laws. Amongst his favourite affirmations is the one he learnt from his
mentor Bob Proctor; "I am so happy and grateful now that money comes to me in increasing quantities through multiple sources on a continuous basis". This affirmation at first looked so unreal, but with consistent and persistent usage of the affirmation things rapidly turned around for the best for me. I would have shared more about the details of how I did it but in case you want to know the details, call +234-8061290548, +234-7044130097.

www.ingramcontent.com/pod-product-compliance
Lightning Source LLC
Chambersburg PA
CBHW051347170526
45166CB00002B/996